...ganized
Religion

An Ex-Monk
Revisits Life's
Basic Questions

Frank Sanitate

Frank Sanitate

Also by Frank Sanitate:

Don't Go to Work Unless It's Fun
  —State-of-the-Heart Time Management

© Santa Barbara Press, 2002

1152 Camino Manadero

Santa Barbara, CA 93111-1063

www.franksanitate.com

ISBN:

  0-9722748-1-2

Library of Congress

  Control Number: 2004094743

Table of Contents

Section 1:

ABOUT THIS BOOK AND THE AUTHOR

Dedication

I dedicate this book to these courageous people:

- Bishop Robinson, who in *Honest To God* allowed his commitment to searching for truth to outweigh his commitment to doctrine.
- Alan Watts, who in *The Book: On the Taboo Against Knowing Who You Are* gives a humbling, freeing and empowering description of the nature of human existence.
- Barbara Marx Hubbard, who in *Birthing the Universal Human* paints a picture of the direction human faith needs to take in this millennium.
- Carl Sagan and Ann Druyan, who in *Shadows of Forgotten Ancestors* comprehensively combine the best of scientific knowledge to give a clear picture of the nature of the universe, the starting point for any viable belief system.

My mind is my own church,
my country is the world,
and my religion is
to do good.

—*Thomas Paine*

Acknowledgements

I acknowledge the many people who have reviewed and given me helpful input on this book: Ron Hansell for his extensive comments, Marianne Brush, Bill Young, Bro. Mike Dundin, FSC, Margaret and Phil Small and Jim Casey.

There were many reviewers of my first edition 6 or 8 years ago. The ones I remember, whose comments I appreciate, are: My sister, Veronica Sanitate Middleton for her extensive comments; my niece, Beth Taylor Hart; Ken Schatz, Barbara Gaughen, Marcia Meier (who suggested I write it in prose rather than dialogue) and several others whom I can't remember!

I acknowledge Ernie and Patty Weckbaugh for editing and packaging the book, and for the typing help of by former assistant, Fury Curtin Cole, and my current assistant, Laura Erickson.

Finally, I thank Barbara Marx Hubbard and Jonathan Robinson for their comments about the book.

Notice

The use of gender specific pronouns for god in this book will be totally random and based primarily on whim. I, of course, have a lot to say about the concept of "god," and neither "he" nor "she" is appropriate for me to use. The use of both randomly may help to break down narrow preconceptions. I will also use "he" sometimes when I should say "he or she," or "man" instead of "humankind" to avoid clumsiness. I have no intention of insulting anyone, but simply to have good language flow.

Also, I will use plural pronouns and adjectives for singular antecedents, because it pleases me (this is not to be construed as a theological principle). If anyone doesn't like this, they can write to Edwin Newman.

Beyond Organized Religion

Chapter 1:

INTRODUCTION

I left home at 18 years of age in September, 1959, to join the Christian Brothers. The Christian Brothers is a Catholic religious order of Brothers dedicated to teaching. It was founded by Jean Baptiste De La Salle, a French priest, in France in 1724. Technically, the order is known as Brothers of the Christian Schools (Fratres Scholarum Christianarum – FSC, which were the initials after my name for 10 years). Their original purpose was to "teach the poor gratuitously." Yes, in case you are wondering, it is one and same group that started Christian Brothers wines and brandy. They sold the company a while back.

I decided to leave the order in late 1969. A year or so before, I decided to give up the fiction that I was still a Catholic. While I was in the order I taught English and religion at St. Joseph's Collegiate Institute in Buffalo, New York. As a religion teacher, I had decided that I was not going to teach anything I didn't really believe in myself. So, I found myself informally re-evaluating what I believed at the end of each year. I would say, "No, I don't believe in this or this anymore, but I still believe in this." I noticed that each year my list of beliefs got shorter and shorter, with my collection of non-beliefs lengthening proportionately. Finally, I realized that calling myself a "liberal Catholic" didn't do it for me anymore – 95 percent of Catholics probably would not have shared the same beliefs that I held at that time. Or more accurately, they still believed things which I no longer believed.

Over the last decade or so, I decided to take a look at my beliefs once again. What is it that I really believe in right now? The inquiry took me into the nature of belief itself: what does "to believe" means? In the process, I wondered how I could possibly have held some of the beliefs I used to hold. It has been a fruitful journey for me, and I want to share some of those fruits with you, hopefully in a way that gives you hope, courage and a firm foundation for yourself.

Actually, the process itself of writing this book got me to think through and more clearly define my beliefs. This is my own little "Summa Theologica," a summation of my own religious/spiritual/theological beliefs. One belief I do have is that everybody should write their own "Summa"! The process is very useful. In fact, this is only the current generation of my thoughts and beliefs. I say "current." I have been writing pieces of this for at least 10 years. These are my thoughts as of this edit. I continue to clarify, refine, adjust, reconsider. They are meant to open an ongoing dialog – within myself, and between you and me. Any belief system worth its salt must be open to on-going re-examination.

Chapter 2:

ABOUT THIS BOOK

My primary purpose is to give you, in bite-size pieces, everything you will ever, ever, ever need to know about theology, god and religion. Fortunately that means it doesn't have to be a very long book! A second purpose, however, is to cut through the crap of useless tomes of theology, encrusted religious practice and paradigm-bound talk about god and to get down to some essentials underlying organized religion. The essentials ought to be common sense, sensible and empowering. I think it achieves this purpose. the most important purpose, though, is to give you a vehicle for formulating, or reformulating or confirming your own thinking about life's most important questions.

I find that most of the popular "spiritual" books of the last decade or so, such as *Conversations with God*, are not empowering to me. They still seem to come from the old paradigm about god as a "he" or "she," which no longer does anything for me. Others are written as parables. I respect these books (unlike fantasy books such as *The Celestine Prophecy*) because their thrust is the same as mine. However, I wanted to write without needing to appeal to any outside authors, but to understand the sacred from looking within, from the context of my own everyday experience.

I now have a very different understanding of "god" than I used to. However, in this and several other chapters, I use the word "god" in the old sense – a being out there who is sort of like us, but mega-everything good. When I talk about god in the chapters of that title, I express a very different idea, which requires a paradigm shift. I suspect that some readers will have a hard time accepting what I say about god until we clear up a lot of other things first such as truth, faith, and so on. So, I speak in the old paradigm until old ideas get cleared up, and then the new paradigm may make more sense.

What could possess me to write a book that challenges dozens of beliefs of millions of people? There are two answers. One answer has to be the same as the one given by Copernicus, Galileo, Darwin and thousands of others: The pursuit of truth. What is "so big," as my 10-year-old would say, about the truth? The truth shall set you free, as Jesus said. The second answer is that I don't really contradict any beliefs. I do challenge them. Beliefs, by their very nature, can't contradict each other because they are stories we make up. You can tell any number of stories you want, and they can all stand. Beliefs don't live in the realm of contradiction; we can speak of "contradiction" only in the realm of fact, data. More on this later.

Finally, don't be fooled by the simplicity in which these ideas are set forth. There is no major question you can ask about life that is not treated and answered here. Of course, the answers are my answers. But truly, all the answers are here. If you have a major question that is not answered, write or call me. I'll give you the answer! Better yet, make up your own! I sometimes take on an authoritarian tone. Don't let it distract you from the primary purpose of this book: to stimulate you to formulate your own thinking.

WHO SHOULD READ THIS BOOK?

This book is primarily for the unwashed. A better name would be the "searchers," either those who once were or those who never were very religious but who are searching. The first group of searchers are the "fallen-away," those like me who were once religiously oriented, but who have given up many of their beliefs and are searching for something to replace them. I used to perceive "fallen-away" as a negative concept, but now I see it as positive. To make it even better let's rename us, the "fallen to," or better, the "leaped to": "There was this huge opportunity to know the truth and I leaped to seize it." The problem with the "leaped to" concept is that we often don't have the sense that we leaped <u>to</u> anything. At best, we feel that we have leaped <u>from</u> something and we are happy to have gotten away, but we don't have a strong sense of having moved into or toward something positive, something we can uphold and be proud of. A big part of the problem is that we have left a community of believers but have not jumped into a new community of "believers in non-belief." In fact, we are not much interested in a new belief system: "You fool me once, shame on you; you fool me twice, shame on me." So, we are left with a vague feeling of dislocation, incompletion and perhaps invalidation. We have not denied god, but we do not have much use for organized religion; and the religions do not have much use for us. We may even still feel tainted as if we really did "fall" or were "unwashed" – concepts that are part of the old belief system. So there it lies, for ten or twenty or ninety years. This book is for those readers. It is preaching to people who have fled the choir – to give you a sense of having leaped to something, of having made a positive move, of being totally capable of formulating your own world-views.

The second group of searchers is the non-believers. However, "non-believer" is self-contradictory. Everyone has beliefs, even if the belief is in non-belief. These can be divided into two categories, both of which should benefit from this book. The first is the Irreverent: those who don't take religion or life too seriously much of the time, but who wouldn't mind some rethinking and illumination – and perhaps some justification for not taking life too seriously! The second group is the Reverent: those who consider themselves spiritual and who would like to deal more openly with questions traditionally commandeered by organized religions. 13

WHO SHOULD NOT READ THIS BOOK

This book is <u>not</u> for true believers or fundamentalists, people with strong religious beliefs. It is probably not even for regular church-goers. I mean it! If you consider yourself as such, you will probably find this book upsetting. I know, because I had some people of strong faith review the first draft, and they were not very pleased with it or me!

This book is written by someone, me, who had a fundamental paradigm shift. If you are clear and sure about your religious beliefs, don't read this – unless you are looking to test the boundaries of your belief system and are willing to be upset a little. If you find yourself threatened as you are reading, a valuable question to ask yourself is: What is being threatened within me? This will help you to clarify the paradigm in which you are operating.

My intention is not to upset anybody. But honestly, several emotions have led me to write:
1. anger
2. desire for the truth
3. love
4. to have some fun

I feel angry because I am upset that so many people have had their lives messed up by belief systems that don't serve them – as happened to me. Not that my belief in Catholicism and Christianity did not benefit me, but I now realize that I can enjoy those benefits without experiencing some of the debilitating drawbacks inherent in that belief system. A better way to say it may be that those beliefs nurtured me into an adolescent phase of spirituality, and I was then ready to move into the adult phase.

The second emotion, related to the first, is the desire for the truth. What so many people say is so, just isn't so. I have come to a much clearer understanding of the nature of knowing, an understanding that was blocked in my old belief system. I have clearer answers to the vital questions, pursued in what is generally known as epistemology: What does "to know" mean? What does "to mean" mean? In short, what is "truth"? Finally, I have formulated some answers that work for me.

The third emotion is love: I want to give something to you. Because the truth sets us free, I have much greater freedom than I had before. This is a gift that I want to share. I believe that this book will help you structure your own thinking.

The fourth emotion, or better, intention, is to have some fun. We need to not take religion, nor life, too seriously. This is not just a cute saying. Humor and laughter perhaps are <u>the</u> fundamental response to life. Lightening up applies to all aspects of life, including religion. If we didn't take religion so seriously, we could then stop killing each other, literally and figuratively. I must admit that I had a lot more fun writing the first (unpublished) edition of this book, but I think this version will be more useful to people. I have also cut down on a lot of the first emotion, anger, as well. However, it may still piss off fundamentalists.

STRUCTURE OF THE BOOK

There are six major sections to this book. They are the major headings in the table of contents, which are:

- **Section 1: About this book and me**
  This is introductory material about the book and me – the section you are reading right now.

- **Section 2: About how we know**
  You can't talk about god unless you talk about talking about god first. That is, we have to look into the nature of knowing, truth and belief first, because talk about god involves belief.

- **Section 3: About the existence and nature of god**
  We need to explore what people mean by "god" and the three major needs that seem to have given rise to talk about god. I then examine each of these needs.

- **Section 4: About how to be in life**
  If we are partially creators of our own lives, how do we go about doing that? This involves looking at happiness, holiness and the meaning of life.

- **Section 5: Miscellaneous stuff** – This is a useful heading for a few other concluding things I want to say.

- **Section 6: A church for the millennium**
  If what I have to say has validity, I wanted to explore how a community of people who held the same beliefs might organize itself and how we might function.

HOW TO READ THIS BOOK

As you will soon see, this is not a book of answers. It may look like a book of answers, but they are only my answers. If you want real answers, look within. That is one premise of this book: we have within ourselves all the resources we need. That is, we have the answers, or we have the ability to get the answers. In fact, since we are sacred, we have the ability to find the resources we need to get everything we want in life. I am simply sharing my answers in the hope that they, or at least the questions, will be useful to you. They are, after all, not <u>my</u> thoughts anyhow but gifts from the universe that simply happened to show up in my head and on paper. Thought uses us as a vehicle to manifest itself is another way of putting it. I suspect that if you are reading this, you are not just a jalopy but a pretty good vehicle yourself.

Think of this as a *Think and Do* book – a title I remember from my elementary school days at St. Margaret Mary Elementary School in Detroit. That is, it really is meant to have you make up your own answers – and, more importantly, make up your own questions. To take an interactive approach, you might do this:

1. Make margin notes of your thoughts as your read: your objections, your "what about this's?" your questions, etc.
2. Since the margins aren't very big, have your own notebook, tape recorder or computer with you as you read, so you are free to put down your thoughts more fully.
3. Allow yourself to follow and write whatever line of thought comes up, even if it has little to do with what you've just read. If you spend two minutes reading and 58 minutes writing, that will be profoundly more useful to you than the reverse.
4. Gather and organize your thoughts and publish your own book! Feel free to send me your thoughts also. I would be happy to enter into dialog with you, if time and interest permit. (Since I have already published *Don't Go to Work Unless It's Fun*, I follow that rule with regard to reading and writing as well.)

The nature of the thought process is that one thought triggers another. Sometimes it triggers two or three thoughts, and then you have to pick which of those thoughts you will follow. What I have tried to do is to pick up all the lines of thought I wanted to pursue, at least somewhere in the book. So you may find that I address a question that comes up for you in another section of the book. But it is really important for you to formulate your questions and answers when they are hot, when they occur. That is much more important than searching around trying to find out what I have to say. My idea of a church is that each of the now six billion or so of us write our own theology, and then we sit down and discuss what we think with great reverence for each other.

The intended result of this book is that you understand more clearly what's in your heart, have greater intensity in your spirituality, greater clarity and precision in your thinking, make a greater contribution with your life, and have fun in the process.

POSSIBLE SUB-TITLES

Here is a list of possible sub-titles for this book that I have thought of at various times while writing it. I share them with you since each of them carries a little of the book's flavor. They also help fulfill the "illusions of grandeur" part of my personality. Most of them are self-explanatory.

- Spirituality for Dummies
- Cults, Religion and Blind Faith: Re-evaluating Your Own Religious Belief Systems
- A Credo for Non-Believers in Credos
- Reflections of a Simple Ex-Monk
- A New Catechism for the Millennium
- The Good News According to Frank
- Toward a Revolution for God (and Against Religion)
- Toward Global Theistic Unity
- God Told Me to Write This Book
- Redeeming the Redeemed
- Re-framing Traditional Religious Beliefs for the Millennium
- When Did We Feed Thee? – A Shocking Revelation About Revelation
- A Spiritual, Anti-religious Treatise
- Shifting the Religion Paradigm
- Bad Things About God (But She Doesn't Care)
- Spirituality Without God – A Reinterpretation of the Universe
- The Simple Summa – I Didn't Know I Knew Everything I Needed to Know
- Everything You Will Ever, Ever Need To Know About God, Religion, and Theology
- From Barbarity to Paradise – An Interim Report
- The "Made-for-TV" Summa Theologica

I also want to thank the many participants in my workshops who have come up with possible titles. I haven't listed all the possibilities, but they helped me narrow it down to the final title.

Chapter 3:

A BRIEF PARTIAL AUTOBIOGRAPHY

I was born the fifth of seven children in Detroit, Michigan, in 1941. My parents, Dominic and Antonette Sanitate, were both immigrants from Italy. My mother was a staunch Catholic who found great solace and support in the church. I attended St. Margaret Mary grammar school, taught by the Sisters of St. Joseph, and St. Joseph's High School, taught by the Christian Brothers.

After graduating from high school, I left home in September, 1959, at 18 years of age to join the Catholic religious order of the Christian Brothers. A religious order is a group of people who join together in community to dedicate their lives to god and to do good works. They generally take vows of poverty, chastity and obedience. Jean Baptiste de LaSalle founded the order several centuries ago for the purpose of teaching the poor gratuitously. This was at a time in France when there was no public education. The Christian Brothers are still teaching today, although they are quite reduced in numbers from 30 years ago when I left, and they are not necessarily teaching the poor. La Salle wrote a set of rules for the order which was based on the monastic rules of, I believe, St. Augustine. There was an inherent conflict in his doing this. The rules were set up for people who remove themselves from the world to live

19

a contemplative monastic life of silence and prayer. However, the purpose of the Brothers was to go into the world to teach others. We followed a monastic rule pretty much for the first one or two years in the order, but after that we gradually dropped the rigors imposed by that rule. As a nickname, we called ourselves "the monks."

The first year or so of religious training is called the novitiate. We had to choose a new name, so I selected Brother Francis Anthony. During that time we lived a strict monastic existence. We got up at five in the morning and had a rigorous daily schedule. We prayed, meditated, attended liturgy, did spiritual reading, attended religious lectures, etc. We generally kept silence except for specific periods of time. When we " broke silence," we were to begin our discussion by saying, "live Jesus in our hearts." The person you were speaking to responded, "forever." We were even encouraged to keep "modesty of the eyes." That is, we were to keep our eyes cast toward the ground. Why would anyone want to live such an existence? The idea was to separate one's self from external things in order to lead an inner spiritual life, focused totally on god.

After that novitiate year, we had four years of college, the first two were in-house, and the last two at Catholic University of America in Washington, D.C. We each chose a secular major and also took a lot of theology courses. The conflict between a monastic rule and trying to live in modern society was sometimes painful. I remember an attractive blonde woman speaking to me as we were walking out of one of our English classes. I wanted to be polite but I remembered the rule of avoiding contact with women. So I tried to walk faster than she was walking to resolve the conflict! She gradually gave up. It was only years later that I could laugh about this incident without being embarrassed by it.

After graduating from college I was assigned to teach at St. Joseph's Collegiate Institute, a college prep high school for boys in Buffalo, New York. I had majored in English, so I taught English classes at various levels. Each of the

Brothers also had a home room class to whom we taught religion. In teaching religion, I did not teach anything that I did not believe myself. I found myself continually re-evaluating my beliefs. Though I didn't do this in a very formal way, I remember looking at my beliefs at the end of each school year. What I noticed was that I kept dropping off more and more of my beliefs. I would say, "I don't believe this and this anymore, but I still believe that." The next year the "that" I believed last year dropped off of this year's list. At first I labeled myself a liberal Catholic, but gradually I admitted to myself that I didn't believe what the majority of Catholics believed. So I didn't call myself Catholic anymore, or even Christian.

In 1969, I took a sabbatical year to study theology and get a master's degree in religious education at Manhattan College. In reviewing that decision, I believe it was a last ditch attempt to find "a wise man," someone who was spiritual but still was living with integrity in the modern world. By integrity I mean not being willing to contradict or deny what one experiences or needs. Unfortunately, I was quickly disillusioned. I attended summer and fall classes, but by November I found myself skipping most of my classes. I even got a job at Bohack's Supermarket, stocking shelves, just to do something different. That only lasted for about three weeks. On the Wednesday before Thanksgiving my manager said, "I'll see you on Friday." Apparently, he didn't understand the concept of Thanksgiving vacation!

It was that this point that I decided to leave the theology program, the Christian Brothers, and teaching. When I told my father that I was leaving the order, he said exactly the same thing to me that he said when I told him I was entering. "Frankie," he said, "you do what you think is best." I realized in later years that I followed his religious pattern since that time, which was to go to church periodically because it was important to our wives. As the years passed, he got more religion, and I got less.

Looking back on the period after leaving the Brothers, I

recognize that it was a difficult period for me. I had gone through a long period of giving up old beliefs, but I did not have any new ones to take their place. It was a time of emptiness and depression. Of course, it took me a while to realize I was depressed. After a couple of years I began psychotherapy with Bob Kronemeyer, which I did for about five years. I remember after one session having decided that it was better to be living than not to be living. I had reached the 51% level – 51% for living, 49% against! I was shocked when I admitted this to myself. What could I have been thinking all those years? That living was not worth it! It was only then that I realized what a depressed state I had been in. After that, I could monitor my growth by saying to myself that it's now 60-40, then 75-25, and so on. I'm pleased to announce that it is now 100% for me! I don't know exactly when I reached that point, but what a blessing to be here!

I have always had the habit of writing or taping my thoughts, but for many years I didn't deal with religious issues or beliefs. In the past ten years or so I decided to revisit my beliefs to determine if I actually believed in anything I used to believe in, or what exactly my beliefs were. As I wrote, the writing began to shape itself into a book. A couple of working titles were *The One Minute Theologian* (compliments of my wife, Terre) and *Don't Go to Church Unless It's Fun*. The latter title was meant to link it to a book I published in 1994, *Don't Go Work Unless It's Fun!* I actually finished this book, I thought, in 1995, but there were three problems. The first was that it was in the form of a catechism, that is, a question and answer format. It was fun because it offered a venue for some great dialogue, but that made for choppy reading. The second was that it was meant to be humorous, but it came out somewhat angry and sarcastic. Both of these things downplayed some insights which I thought were valuable. The third problem was that I gave the draft to several friends to read, and the response was "whelming." (Figure it out!) So I decided to rewrite it in a prose format; hence, what you're reading now. In re-reading the earlier book, I was surprised at the sharp edge there was to it. However, it was very useful for me to write that book. First, I think it helped me to purge some feelings of anger I still had about my earlier experiences. Secondly, I must have edited the book about five times, and each time I clarified my thinking a little more. I am using the chapters as a basis for this book, and I am eager to see how my thoughts further develop as I dictate them. I hope they are as interesting to you as they are to me!

Talking about the writing process brings something to memory from my studies of the Augustan era in English literature: the metaphor of the spider and the bee. The spider wove his web by spinning it out from inside of himself. The bee went outside of itself to gather honey from flower to flower. The first produces from going within; the second from going without. Although it is much more attractive to be a bee, I've always been a spider. That is, rather than finding out what other people think first, I have always preferred looking inward to see what's so. I remember my English literature mentor, Father Rooney, saying, "Brother Francis, most students I have to encourage to do some thinking for themselves. You, I have to encourage to go out to do some research in secondary sources."

This is the way I have looked at religion as well. Like Thomas the doubter I want to see for myself. What is it that I experience, that I see? I spent my first twenty years of life being indoctrinated from without in Catholicism. I then realized that the main person you have to trust is yourself. Otherwise, you're trapped into trying to figure out what this theologian thinks about what that theologian thinks about what the other theologian thinks. It gets pretty hard to figure out what's true. Besides, I didn't have each of them in front of me to ask, "What do you mean when you say this? Why do you say that?" Perhaps these thoughts helped me to formulate Sanitate's first principal: If you can't know something, it doesn't matter. More on that later.

That is why I've taken such great pleasure in formulating this book. It all comes from the question: what do I think? It provided the space for a lot of fresh thinking, for me, on life's basic questions. Perhaps that gives a signal to you as well – use my thoughts to stimulate you to formulate your own thoughts on these questions. As Jesus said, "The kingdom of god is within."

Finally, I want to share a history of breakthrough moments in my theological development. I will present them chronologically with 1 or 2 year margin of error!

• Age 14 - Fr. Conroy, our pastor, used to have some of my elementary school friends (boys) give him rubdowns. None of them ever reported anything more happening. Then later in high school, "little Joe," a Christian Brother, used to rub up against me in class, with a "stiffy" under his robe. He accosted me in the cloak room once, but I got annoyed with what he was trying to do and left. I realized the humanness of the clergy, and that theological theory and practice didn't necessarily match.

• Age 18 - When I was in the novitiate, I mentioned to some Brothers an earlier incident which occurred when I was an altar boy. The priest dropped a communion wafer on the rug, and asked me to get a little hand towel to put over it. When he came back after Mass and lifted the towel, the wafer was gone! If you believed the wafer was actually Jesus, as I did, then certainly it could disappear on its own. But Brother Thomas Basilian laughed in great disbelief. Of course, I may not have noticed that the priest picked up the wafer first and then put a towel on the spot. This never even occurred to me. The incident brought into question the whole realm of belief in magic, miracles, the breaking the laws of nature and common sense that so many of church teachings required.

• Age 19 - I came to the vital distinction that when people talked about the Church, they were talking about how it should be, not what it actually was!

• Age 20 - As a college sophomore I remember asking Brother Augie Tom what Protestants were looking for in studying the *Bible*, and he answered, "the truth." I had meant that question seriously. I came to realize that I had totally discounted all other religions and people who were not Catholics.

• Age 21 - We read a book called *God and the Ways of Knowing* and were supposed to write a paper on it. The title of my paper was *God and My Ways of Knowing.* The point of it was that I was tired of studying what other people taught and wanted to explore what I thought (the story of my life!)

• Age 22 - As a senior in college I had the thought, "why would god choose such a god-awful thing as circumcision as a sign of the covenant with the Jews?" That reminds me: Moses came down from the mountain and told Aaron about the covenant. Aaron says, "Let me get this straight. The Arabs get all the lands with oil under them, and we get to cut off the tips of our penises?" I apologize; I had to throw that in! So I wrote a paper, *The Source of Circumcision as Sign of the Covenant.* It turns out that the practice of circumcision was around long before Moses climbed the mount, and the Jews thought it would commandeer loyalty if they said, "OK, this is the reason we are going to say we are doing it from now on." Similarly, Christmas was placed on Dec. 25 because is was a time of pagan feasts, not because the *Bethlehem Gazette* said, "Dec. 25, 0000 - Jesus Born Today!" I learned in a scripture class that, as with so much else in the *Bible*, human actions and customs came first and "revelation" followed – exactly the opposite of what I had always thought.

• Age 24 - In a graduate theology class at the University of Detroit I did a paper on *Does the Devil Exist?* There didn't seem to be any evidence for it other than biblical say so, but at the time I thought: If we can assign no external agent as a source of evil, then we could just as easily do away with an external agent as the source of good. In other words, if we do away with the devil, what will prevent us from doing away with god? I wasn't ready to go that far at that time.

• Age 29 - Just before I left the Brothers, I began a graduate theology program at Manhattan College. As I said earlier, I was looking for a member of a religious order – not successfully – who was a fully alive, fully functioning human being. I took a class from Gabriel Moran, then a well-known Christian Brother and theologian. For a final test he allowed us to submit 5 questions to him ahead of time, out of which he would select two for our individual final exam! One of my questions was: "Where do people who talk about god get their information?" I had the theory that they made it up. Unfortunately, he did not select this question for my final test. (Mike Keegan, a friend who also was just about to leave the Brothers submitted the question: "What is the dividing line between Brooklyn and Queens!") I concluded that since I couldn't find the wise man, I would have to become one myself.

• Age 29 - As I left the Brothers, I said that if one were going to live a life of poverty, chastity and obedience, one ought to be living and working in with the poor in Harlem or in a prison, not in a middle-class suburban college prep high school. I wasn't ready for that I also knew I wasn't a Catholic, doubted I was a Christian, and wondered if I was a theist.

• Age 49 – I started to write my thoughts on religion and belief, which eventually turned into this book.

Section 2:

ABOUT HOW WE KNOW

Chapter 4:

TRUTH

What is truth?

Before addressing the question, "What is faith?" we need to address the question, "What is truth?" These are big questions, and they are interrelated. Truth is often used synonymously with reality: truth is "what's so." That brings up an even more fundamental question: how do we, I, **know** what's so? How do I know, perceive reality?

So I am going to take you on an excursion in this chapter to explore these interdependent questions:

1. What is perception: How do we know what's so, what's out there?
2. What is reality: What <u>is</u> so; what is reality; what is out there?
3. What is truth?
4. What is faith? (I will discuss this question in the next chapter.)

1. What is perception?

To explore perception, I invite you to take three tests on the following page. You are at an advantage because you may have seen these before or because you have a longer time than I give my seminar participants to look at them to come up with an answer. However, let's see how well you do:

1. Read what you see below out loud:

a
bird
in the
the hand

2. Count the number of times the letter "f" appears in this statement and write down your answer:

Finished files are the results of years of scientific study combined with the experience of many years.

Number of "f"s: _____

3. What do you see below?

I hope you have tried to answer all three questions honestly. I also hope that you noticed the extra "the" in the first test. Secondly, I hope you came up with the number six for the second test. Finally, I hope you saw the word "fly" in the third test.

Selective Perception

Usually, people get caught on at least one of these examples. They don't accurately perceive what's there. Why? The answer is selective perception. That is, we really don't perceive "what's out there," but we selectively perceive what's out there based on a set of rules, assumptions, beliefs we maintain within ourselves. This is what a paradigm is – a set of rules, assumptions, beliefs through which we perceive and from which we operate. It is a mental model we have of the way things are, and it determines what we selectively let in or keep out of our perception.

In the first test, the assumption is that we already know this phrase, since we have heard or read it before. Also, we have a model of "triangle" in our head; we "see" a triangle there and become distracted. Many of us don't really read what's there. We read what's in our memory and miss seeing the extra "the." In the second test many people come up with the answer "three." They miss the letter "f" in the word "of." (Sometimes they catch only one or two of them.) Why do we miss the "of's"? When we say the word "of" and listen to the sound, it is actually a "v" sound. So, some of us use our auditory sense rather than our visual sense in counting "f's" in the sentence. The model or paradigm from which we work prevents us from seeing what's there. Finally, if you don't see the word "fly" in the third test, it's because you are trying to make sense out of the black marks rather than the spaces between the marks. That's where the letters are. There are two paradigms working here: first, we generally look for meaning in the black rather than the space that surrounds the black. Secondly, when we read print, letters are usually in black and spaces are white. Again, the rules or model in our head determine what we perceive. The bottom line is that we don't really perceive what's out there; we selectively perceive what we expect to be out there based on models or rules which we operate from.

You may think that these are just some psychological gimmicks, but if we go to the fundamental level of sight itself, we find that even the act of seeing is based on rules. We think that seeing is a "natural" process, but it is not. It depends on our having learned a whole set of rules as infants. If we don't learn those rules, we can't see and understand what is before us. It is extremely difficult for someone born blind who regains the physical capacity for sight in adulthood to come to be able to see. They must very slowly and with great difficulty learn the rules which we're not even conscious of and which we take for granted. Many studies with humans and animals corroborate this. For example, kittens brought up in an environment of horizontal lines, bump into chair and table legs when put in normal situations because they cannot perceive vertical things. The rules or paradigm in which they operate work only for a horizontal world. You can get a sense of how this works the next time you're in an elevator which has Braille numbers. Close your eyes and touch each number to see if you can distinguish between them. Most people can't because our fingers are not sensitive enough to perceive the differences, whereas a blind person can readily perceive them. Our fingers haven't learned the rules of "fine perception" yet.

If you were tripped up by one of the tests above, your self-confidence may be lessened a little. This is good! We need to trust our own senses, but have a little humility in doing so. We don't really perceive what's out there; we perceive what we perceive is out there. Disconcerting as this may seem, on a day-to-day level, differences in perceptions of physical reality don't generally make too much difference. It is not an accident that when I use an umbrella because I perceive it is raining, everybody else is carrying an umbrella too (or would like to be). I perceive it is raining, and lo and behold it is. Most of our everyday physical experience plays out as if there were a totally objective reality out there which is totally clear to everyone.

Why is it that we don't perceive everything accurately? That is, why do we need rules which allow some things into our perception and don't allow others? Simply, there is too much going on out there for us to be aware of everything. Our reticular system receives eight million bits of information per second. We can't possibly be aware of everything that's going on, so we need a set of rules to determine what we let in and what we filter out. The problem is that because of these rules we also shut out information. This is what I call the paradox of learning: we can't learn anything unless we have a model or paradigm which blocks out information so that we can focus. Yet we can't learn anything new or outside of that model unless we give up or shift the model. To perceive anything we need to shut out information, and to grow in knowledge we need to let in information!

2. What is Reality?

As you can see from what I have just said, there is no "objective" answer to the question, "What is reality?" Even if there were an objective "out there," it is always going to be perceived by somebody (or else we wouldn't be talking about it, and it wouldn't matter then). Reality is a combination of what's out there (data, fact) and how I perceive and interpret it. This distinction between what happens and my interpretation of what happens is the most valuable learning I got out of the est seminars many years ago. Although on the physical level our differences in perception generally don't make too much difference on a daily basis (other than in the realm of scientific research), on the psychological level they make a profound difference. In our human interactions we bring a psychological set of rules which determine what and how we perceive, and we create an interpretation of the situation based on those rules. Although they are based on what's "out there," they are our interpretations, which are subject to error.

Here is a real-life example: I would sometimes clean the kitchen while my wife Terre was away. When she came back, she didn't even seem to notice this wonderful deed that I had done, and never acknowledged it. This was upsetting to me because this is how I would win my mother's approval when I was a young boy. She would come home and say, "Oh, what a good boy. You cleaned the kitchen." So I finally talked to Terre about it. She said that she did notice the clean kitchen. But when she was a little girl, and her mother cleaned something that Terre was supposed to have done, Terre took it as a criticism: "You didn't clean things up, so I had to do it." So, how was she going to thank me for doing something that criticized her? Even though we were looking at the same facts or data – Frank cleaned the kitchen – we came up with different stories or interpretations of it. Then the story, interpretation or assumption we make about the situation generates a feeling or emotion, and we act based on that feeling.

Notice that there are usually four steps in the sequence of human behavior:

1.   Something happens (fact, data)
2.   We make up a story or interpretation about it.
3.   Emotions are aroused, based on the story.
4.   We act based on the emotions.

Another example: I am driving and someone cuts me off. The "someone cut me off" part is already a subjective interpretation I make up about what objectively or factually happened. If I were factually describing the situation, I would say something like: "I was driving in the right lane at 60 miles per hour and a car from the lane on my left pulled in front of me with 10 feet of space between our cars. I put on my brakes." When I say, "cut me off," that implies the driver was trying to do something to harm me. Or, he did something without caring about consequences to me. Or, he was too careless to even know I was there. These are all stories or interpretations I make up about the data, and then feelings flow from the story – I get angry. Then actions might flow from the feelings. (I will let you use your imagination about what actions might come forth.) If I weren't making up this story or interpretation, then I would have simply braked or swerved without any emotion, just as naturally as we turn on the windshield wipers when it starts to rain. If you have emotion in a situation with another person, you are definitely making up a story, an interpretation, about the data.

Where does the story or interpretation come from? From the first example, we can see that they come from our past history. When I say "past history" though, that is a combination of several things: our personal past experiences, the influences of others - our culture and our parents - our genes and our bodily states.

Concerning the first two, we formulate all of our fundamental attitudes about life during childhood. We inherit many of them from others – our parents, our culture, our siblings, our peers. This is why the unexamined life is not worth living. Some of us are still operating based on unquestioned attitudes we have had since toddlerhood, and from life decisions we made perhaps as early as then! Since these inherited attitudes are beliefs, I will discuss belief more fully in the next chapter on **Faith**, and why we need to re-examine these beliefs in the chapter on **Growing Up**. I will also discuss the need to stand back and question our beliefs and belief systems. We need to challenge the assumptions, the paradigm from which we perceive and interpret what's around us, especially when they don't seem to be serving us.

Concerning the last two, I have two brief comments: After reading the book *Genome*, I am amazed at how much of what we turn out to be - including our perceptions - are genetically determined. People with Attention Deficit Disorder just don't see things the way others do. They do not process information the way other people do. The "bodily states" idea is illustrated by the saying, "depression is a chemical flaw, not a character flaw." So the perceptions of someone who is depressed may be largely influenced by an imbalance in chemicals.

In summary, "reality" is a combination of fact, data – what's out there – and the story or interpretation I make up about the data. We all live in "reality," but it is "our" reality. So, the concept of reality is a little shaky. First of all, we selectively perceive what's out there. Then, we invent an interpretation of what we perceive. If this isn't disconcerting enough, listen to what Einstein has to say: "Physical concepts are free creations of the human mind and are not, however it may seem, uniquely determined by the external world." All that stuff like atoms and quarks and muons are something physicists make up! They don't make it up out of thin air (unless, of course, they are studying rarified atmosphere!). There is "something" out there, but they construct stories or explanations which are free creations of their minds.

Isn't this a little frightening: that we all invent our own

reality, our own universe, and then act based on that invention? Yes and no. The negative part is clear: Some "realities" created by individuals in the human community have bad consequences: racism, nationalism, money as an end in itself, scarcity of time, etc. These can lead to terrible consequences like substance abuse, child/spouse-beating, etc. On the other hand, we are not isolated beings. We are born into, grow up in, live with and are buried by a human community. That's why it's useful to "compare notes" with our fellow travelers. We all grow up with unique genes, in a unique environment and with very different experiences, so we necessarily bring different points of view and interpretations to what we perceive. The more we share our perceptions and interpretations, the closer we get to "objective reality," or "truth." The faster we come to recognize the subjectivity and limitations of both our perceptions and the interpretations we make about them, the more productively we operate as a society. Together we create a richer, more accurate picture of what's "out there" and what it takes to move forward together.

3. What is Truth?

What is truth? We can now answer that in two ways. In the first way it is used is as a synonym for reality. It is the underlying "what's so." As I have just finished discussing what's so – reality – is a combination of what's out there and my interpretation of it. Seen from this point of view, there is no "ultimate" truth. Truth is simply the shared combination of human perceptions. What does "ultimate truth" mean anyhow?

The second, simpler way we have for the word "truth" is: When we speak what we know is so. Truth has to do with what we **say** about what's so out there. Truth is accurately reporting what we perceive to be so in the realm of fact or data. For example, when we apply the label "truth" to fact or data – what is verifiable – we would say things like: water freezes at 32 degrees Fahrenheit, or, Sosa hit a home run today, or my name is Frank. If I deny these things, then I am not telling the truth.

When I make an interpretation – a judgment, belief, assumption, evaluation or conclusion - about one of these things (e.g., it is *good* that water freezes at 32 degrees), that statement is neither true nor not true. Truth doesn't have to do with interpretations. It only applies to the realm of data. The problem comes when we try to claim that our interpretation are "true," rather than simply acknowledging that it is an interpretation and therefore a belief. If you preface every belief with the statement "I believe . . . ," you are always telling the truth. Otherwise, beliefs themselves don't have anything to do with truth or not truth. "Truth" is not a label appropriate for interpretations, only for data or fact.

If only people got this distinction, it would eliminate a lot of trouble in our lives. We would stop fighting over whether beliefs are "true." We would accept the relativity of all beliefs. We would then move to the more appropriate question concerning belief: how **useful** is it? More of this in the next chapter.

Summary

However, to understand what we mean by "what's so," we need to understand three fundamental areas:

1. Perception: We don't really perceive what's out there.We selectively perceive what's out there based on aset of assumptions, rules or beliefs - the paradigm -out of which we operate.
2. Reality: Reality is a combination of fact, data – what's out there – and the story or interpretation we make up about it. To understand what's so, we need to recognize that our knowledge is relative, not absolute. We need to distinguish between fact and the interpretations, stories or beliefs we make up about fact.
3. Truth: On one level truth is a synonym for "reality" or "what's so". On a second level, truth means honestly reporting fact or data, and honestly reporting our beliefs as belief.

Chapter 5:

FAITH

What is faith?

From the last chapter we see that reality is a combination of what is out there and the interpretation we make of it. The interpretations we make can also be called a story, an opinion, a belief, etc. For me, faith simply means an interpretation we make about life itself. I use the word synonymously with belief.

Yet, people use the word faith in several ways. Let's explore the seven uses of the word, the ways in which people speak of faith, that I have distinguished so far.

Types of faith

Faith can mean:

1. A belief or group of beliefs about life which are fundamental and to which we have a strong emotional attachment. This kind of belief is the story we make up about the meaning of life itself. For example: "I believe that life is meaningful" or "I believe in karma."

2. A moral belief. This is a judgment that something about human behavior is good or bad, right or wrong. For example: "I believe that abortion is wrong."

3. A hope for something in the future. For example: "I believe in an after-life" or "I believe IBM stock will go up."

4. A trust in someone. For example: "I believe in my son" or "I believe in my CPA."

5. A trust in someone as a leader. For example: "I believe in Mohammed."

6. A belief in what somebody else says. For example: "I believe Jesus rose from the dead."
"Why?"
"Somebody said so, and I believe them."

7. A group of beliefs shared by a group of people. For example: "I am of the Buddhist faith" or "I believe in Taoism." This really is a combination on numbers 1, 5 and 6. It is believing what several people or a community of people say, about what a great leader said (and did) about life. A tradition is established as the community passes along teachings (and inevitably changes them).

There are probably other ways people use the word "faith," but these are the major ones. If we look at what is common in all of these types of belief, we see that they are all stories, stories that we make up or that others have made up about reality. At first blush, this may seem to trivialize the concept of faith or belief – calling it a "story." In modern usage "story" generally means fiction, something that did not happen in real life. But on a more fundamental level, everything we say about life is a story. As discussed in the last chapter, "story" is the nature of everything that we perceive. We make up interpretations or stories: it is raining, there are only three "f's" in the statement in the previous chapter, a UFO is coming, Julius Caesar existed, Julius Caesar was a great king, life is meaningful, abortion is wrong, Abraham is our father, etc. Each of the seven levels above is a story we make up about reality. Some of these may be very good stories, but they are still interpretations or stories. The task of life is to get rid of bad stories and make up good ones.

What constitutes a good story? A good story is one that is functional, one that is useful, one that serves us. When I perceive that it is raining and as a result I use an umbrella and don't get wet, that is a good story. If the stock market crashes and I say, "my life is ruined," and I jumped out a window; that is a bad story. Some stories work in one sense and don't work in another sense. If the story "abortion is wrong" helps people who don't want children to use birth control, that is a good story. If it causes someone to bomb an abortion clinic, it is a bad story. As I said in the last chapter, the word "truth" is not a good word to use when talking about beliefs, because we then get into fights as to whose truth is truer, mine or yours. Truth applies to fact or data. A better question is about our faith or beliefs is: who's story works better? Which one creates a better, more harmonious me, and a better, more harmonious world? Faith, belief, must be in the service of life, and not the other way around. While growing up (a process I am still going through), I thought it was the opposite: faith is paramount and absolute. No matter how miserable it made your life and the lives of others, you couldn't question it. A good story, belief is one that serves life.

When we look at truth, knowing, and belief in this way, we also have to question the concept of "proof." When someone tries to "prove" their story is true, they summon up evidence to support it. Yet every story has evidence behind it. "Even the devil can quote scripture to his own perdition," the *Bible* says. Many people thought Hitler told a good story about the way things are and should be. I was amazed at how much equanimity the Heavenly Gate cult members seemed to have, shortly before they committed suicide in the '90s. What these things tell me is that we often don't know the real motivations that drive us, and so we create plausible stories to justify them. The belief often comes first, and then we garner evidence to support it (and, of course, don't notice evidence that contradicts it). In short, anyone can "prove" their point of view, their beliefs, but that doesn't mean there are no other points of view for which evidence can be gathered as well.

What this line of thinking leads me to is that there is no "reason" for our beliefs. We can always make up reasons to rationalize or justify beliefs, but ultimately that means we can just as easily say that there is <u>no</u> fundamental reason for any belief. Let me take that back; there is a fundamental reason for every belief, and that reason is: I <u>choose</u> this belief. This is the fundamental answer to the question of why anyone holds any belief: Why do you follow Hitler? Why you follow Jesus? Why do you follow your own counsel? The answer for all three is: because I <u>choose</u> to.

In addition to being able to find "reasons" for any particular belief because we choose to, we generally choose <u>not</u> to search out or let in any thoughts or evidence that contradicts the belief. So no matter how many reasons we can come up with for any particular belief, it's still fundamentally a question of choice or decision: I choose to believe this because I choose to believe this. Yet when I ask the question, "why do I choose one belief over another?" the best answer I can come up with is: it feels right, it feels good, my experience corroborates it, it seems to fit. But, bottom-line, it is a decision – I choose to believe this because I choose to believe this.

This thinking might seem to take away any firm ground to stand on. Yet, on a deeper level it puts us on the bedrock of what it means to be human. Although I will take this discussion up later, I want to say now that this is what makes us "gods," or godly: We get to choose our beliefs simply because we choose them, because we say so. Our word creates our reality: "in the beginning was the word, and without the word there was nothing that is." I am godly because I say, "this is so because I say so." However, there are currently over six billion of us for whom this is true. In order to live in this world it is useful to compare notes with others who are saying what's so, because they just might have a better story than ours. Or, they simply may have a different story than ours, since they come from a different point of view. We are not godly in isolation, but as a human community.

I remember writing a long time ago that error is the absence of truth. When we err, we have the truth, but just not enough of it. In other words, when people thought the world was flat, they had evidence for it. What they experienced was valid, true, but the conclusion that the earth was flat was not valid. Gradually they came to have more truth, more knowledge, perhaps from looking at vast panorama from a mountain top and starting to see the curvature of the earth. Ultimately, when ships circumnavigated the globe, this was more information to add to their early store of information, so they decided that "the earth is round," was a better story than the one made up originally. They had data, evidence, which was valid, but there was more data out there which changed the story or interpretation or conclusion once they obtained that data. This is why, as a human community, we need to compare notes.

Is one belief, then, as good as another? On one level yes, and on another no. One belief is as good as another since the reason for my beliefs is the same as yours: because I choose that belief. I can't fault you for choosing what you believe, since you're acting the same way I'm acting. On the other hand, one belief is not as good as another because some people have more experience in the area of their beliefs than others. I would rather listen to a dentist about tooth care than a bricklayer. I would rather listen to someone who lived in Uganda to evaluate our government's policy toward that country, than to someone who can't even locate it on a map. So, clearly, every belief is open to questioning, to get to the facts or data underlying the belief: Why do you believe that?

Beliefs represent underlying values

To further refine it, the question, "Why do you believe that?" is really not the most powerful question we can ask about a belief. The reason is simple: we can find evidence to support virtually any belief. A more important question to ask, then, is, "Why is this belief important to you?" That enables us to get to the value underlying the belief.

For example, if I ask why you believe in a god, you may come up with a multitude of reasons, evidence. But if I ask why the belief is important to you, you might say something like, "If there were no god, life would be meaningless." The next question that might then come up for me might be, "If life were meaningful without the existence of a god, would it still be important to you to believe in a god?" For me, the answer is no. For others, there may still be other values underlying the belief.

We have a strong emotional attachment to our fundamental beliefs, so nobody likes to have them questioned. If I said, further, "Life is not meaningful," you probably would get upset. Why? Because it is a fundamental belief, it is a starting point for you (and for me as well, by the way). When I ask, "why is it important that is life meaningful?" you may not be able to go back any further to a more fundamental answer. You say, "It just is." It is an affirmation, a declaration, a choice. Belief is a choice we make about life. Each belief represents a fundamental value for us. If someone else has the opposite view, it challenges the world we live in, challenges our values. Writing this book is a matter of integrity for me. Why is integrity a value? It just is. It is the way I choose to be.

Breakthroughs occur when we are able to see through a belief we thought was fundamental to the value that underlies that belief. Sometimes we learn that we can have the value without hanging on to the belief. I am reminded of Charles Lamb's **A Dissertation on Roast Pig**. In ancient times man's hut caught fire and accidentally roasted his pet pig inside. When he touched the pig and licked his fingers, he discovered that roast pig tasted very good. After that, every time people wanted to have roast pig they put a pig inside a hut and burned it down! The belief that you had to put a pig inside of a hut to roast it got them roast pig but lost them a lot of huts. When somebody challenges your belief, it may seem like they're telling you that roast pig is no good. You think, "How stupid! This person must never have tasted a roast pig!" But maybe they're telling you that you don't have to burn down your hut to roast one.

The reason we need to question beliefs is that we may be able to have both the roast pig and a standing hut. In other words, when our beliefs are questioned or when we are sincerely interested in exploring other's beliefs, we get to learn that we can have the value that underlies our belief without having to cling to the belief itself. In addition, we get to have more than the one value we are protecting; we get to have other values as well. If you step back and look at it, it's not that you don't value standing huts; you just like roast pig more. So we need to look for bigger beliefs that encompass **all** of our values in a harmonious way – what would it take to have the roast pig and to keep the hut as well? We all value the same things, generally, but we place higher priorities on one value over the other. In addition, questioning beliefs helps us to pierce through surface values to more fundamental ones. For example, you may say that money is a value to you. Why? It allows you freedom. Is freedom a value for you? Yes. Why? It just is. Is it possible, once we see that freedom is the value, that we might see more clearly where money actually serves freedom and where it inhibits it. Perhaps if we all questioned the value of money in our lives, we would have a more equitable world without sacrificing freedom.

In discussing the relativity of faith or belief, it may seem that I am making it unimportant. There is a sense in which it is unimportant, but there is also sense in which it is very important. Our beliefs are unimportant when they get in the way of respecting and loving others. Beliefs aren't important; people are. Life is important. Belief must be in the service of life. On the other hand, belief is absolutely essential for human life. We all have to create stories about what the universe is about, otherwise we would be incapacitated. Our little views and our world views allow us to move forward in life. If we didn't have them we would be like animals simply trying to sustain our lives and procreate. It is highly important to have beliefs, in fact, to search out beliefs that empower us – that give us joy and delight in moving forward in the world. So, be passionate about your beliefs if in fact they create passion in you, but don't let your beliefs get in the way of being passionate about others and about life. And don't be afraid to challenge beliefs – yours and others' – when they seem to be shortchanging other values or life itself.

Summary

For me, faith simply means an interpretation we make about life itself. I use the word synonymously with belief. When we speak of "faith" we usually mean one of the seven ways in which we use the word (listed previously). What is common about the uses of the word is that they are all stories or interpretations we make up about what's so, which contain an underlying value.

The reason behind any belief is not the evidence that supports it — evidence can be found to support any belief — but that we <u>choose</u> to believe. There may be very compelling evidence to make that choice, but it is still a choice. To make free decisions, it is helpful to challenge beliefs, both ours and others', by asking, "Why is this belief important?" We then can discover and affirm the underlying value of the belief. We also become open to better, more inclusive choices or stories about what's so.

Faith is absolutely essential to make our lives meaningful. In fact, it is precisely what we do to interpret life, give it substance, invent its meaning. However, no belief is absolute; all are relative and are a matter of choice. The question to ask about a belief is not whether it is true or not, but whether, or to what degree, the belief is useful. Beliefs must be in the service of life rather than vice-versa.

Chapter 6:

REVELATION

What is revelation? Should we believe in revelation?

When we understand that faith is a story we make up about what's out there, it simplifies the concept of revelation. Revelation means that someone says that certain things have been revealed to them by god, gods, spirits, the deceased, angels, etc. – beings "out there." We believe what the person says because we believe in that person. However, how are we to know whether:

1. These beings who are doing the revealing, in fact, exist.
2. They communicated something to this individual.
3. The individual is accurately reporting what was communicated.
4. Those who are passing the story on are accurately reporting what the previous person said, each in their own turn.

I will discuss the first point in later chapters. Assuming for now that there actually is "somebody," a god, out there, all revelation is based on the fact that somebody (or their followers) tells us it happened to them. They tell us that something was revealed to them by the gods and ask us to believe it is true. When we try to understand revelation, it is impossible to distinguish the facts, what actually happened to the person, from the interpretation that person made about what they were experiencing. Then, it is impossible to separate out the interpretations each person who in turn received the story made of the original story. Take Jesus, for instance. It has been 80 generations since Jesus was here (I presume a generation is 25 years.) It's like the parlor game where someone passes on a story to the next person and so on until you get to the 80th person: "God told us this; pass it on." Even if you use only three or four people the story gets very garbled in the transmission. Most of the major religions in the world began long ago in history. So we have to deal with not only what the original storyteller told us, but the long tradition of other story-tellers who repeat the story and perhaps embellished it. The truth is that we are not believing what "god" revealed; we are believing a story that some guy tells us, which some guy told him, etc. "Some guy" is, perhaps, putting it bluntly; yet, saying "a divinely appointed messenger" means the same thing. We believe others who believe others who believe in a self-appointed emissary of god. One may say, "no, these people were not self-appointed, but they were appointed by god." But who says they were appointed by god? Answer: They do. Just because you say god reveals something to you doesn't mean it's necessarily true. Or, conversely, we all can just as legitimately say that god reveals things to us all.

What complicates "revelation" is that it is not a story we hear for the first time as adults. Most of us have been brought up with these stories as part of our upbringing by our family, our community, our church, our culture. So it is hard for us to step outside of all this, and to rationally evaluate the stories we've received during childhood, much of which we may have held as fact since then. We have a lot of emotional and often un-examined commitments to these stories. That is why in the process of maturing we need to step back and re-examine our beliefs.

Another complication is that it's not as if we've only had an oral tradition for 60 generations. We do have a *Bible* and a *Talmud* and *Koran* and so on. When the story is written down, people reverence these books because of the "revealed" stories in them. However, I can just as irreverently say, "some guy said it and some other guy wrote it down; so what?" The fact that it is written and that people have believed it for centuries doesn't necessarily add anything to its credibility. A lot of people believed in slavery even after slavery was abolished. A lot of people believed in Arian supremacy in the 1930s and 1940s. Some still do. A lot of people today believe they have the right to tell you what to do with the fetus in your body. A lot of people believe the king has clothes on. This is why it is important to examine beliefs even when many people believe them, even when they're written. This is especially necessary when these beliefs divide the human community rather than unite it. We need to take responsibility for our beliefs. We need to admit that we choose these beliefs either because we have examined them and chose them, or because we refuse to examine them and thus choose them unconsciously.

It has been 40 years since I studied the Old Testament in college, but I believe I remember something about there being four different literary strands that went into the Pentateuch - the first five books of the Old Testament. It wasn't just one story from one writer. And I hear of current controversies about how few of the statements given as direct quotes made by Jesus can actually be attributed to him (even though they are printed in red ink in deluxe versions of the *Bible*.) I understand that the gospel of John came out in 90 AD, 60 years or two generations after Jesus died. How well could those people have remembered? And so on. Fundamentalists Christians don't want to hear anything about biblical scholarship: don't confuse me with the facts! But all of us are subject to some unquestioned beliefs in many areas of life. Do you know exactly what you believe and why you believe it? What clear data do you have to substantiate your beliefs? Most of us get caught up in the rush of everyday living and forget to ask basic questions. Most of the time our beliefs serve us just fine, but when they don't we would just as soon not question beliefs because to do so is threatening.

Questioning beliefs is very tricky. I want to be rigorous in questioning my own beliefs, but gentle in questioning the beliefs of others. That's my intention, anyhow. My <u>feeling</u>, on the other hand, often is to want to bash others over the head with my beliefs! On the intellectual level I know I should be gentle because I do reverence others, but on the emotional level I get annoyed because their beliefs are not my beliefs! When you start challenging others' beliefs, they get defensive and thus are not in the place where they can openly examine them. Socrates got himself into big trouble over this!

The bottom-line about revelation is that we are just listening to what some guy said they found out, or what they say some other guy found out. Trying to get back to what Jesus or Mohammed or Moses or Buddha actually said and actually did is a useless inquiry. I didn't always think this way. In fact, as I mentioned earlier, I remember that as a sophomore in college I was sure that we Catholics had cornered the market on truth. I asked Brother Augie Tom who was getting his doctorate in theology, "what are the Protestants who study the *Bible* looking for?" He wisely answered, "truth." This was a revelation (good word to use in this chapter) to me. I must have thought unconsciously that anyone who wasn't a Catholic was an idiot or brainless or actually malevolent. That one word answer helped me come to realize that we are all equals in playing the game of discovering the truth, and that, contrary to what I had grown up believing, Catholics had no better a handle on it than anyone else.

I bring this up because at that point in my life I was thinking that I might go into studying scripture, so that I could find out <u>exactly</u> what Jesus said. And if I knew that, then I would know the truth. However, it is very difficult to discern what Jesus actually said, for reasons I've described. Even if I did know what he said, it is simply what one man says, which has to be measured against what every other man says, especially myself. Thinking about this, and about an after life, and about whether there is a separate god-being out there, I developed Sanitate's First Principal, the first of the Great Self-Evident Truth/Beliefs. I will reveal these Truth/Beliefs to you periodically, and in case you miss any of them, I will summarize them at the end. Here is the first: if you can't know or find out something for sure, then it doesn't matter. If you can't know what Jesus actually said, or whether there is life after death, or if there is one god and Mohammed is his prophet, then it doesn't matter. Why spend life in pursuit of what's impossible to know? It doesn't make difference in how we should live our life anyhow.

Whom should we follow?

But isn't it possible that some people, a great religious leader in particular, had some special insights or experiences more profound than ours, and that we should listen to him or her? Perhaps their experience is more profound than ours, but going back to my first principal, they ought to be able to point the way so that we can experience what they've experienced. If they can't, or if they claim that they have some special experience which is not available to us, then that's something we can't experience or know. And if we can't know it, it doesn't matter. You may say, "well, maybe they have a better grasp of life because of those experiences." That may be true, but if it is something that I cannot experience, if it can't be part of my life, why should I try to live their life? I have to live my life; it's the only life I have. I want to listen to others, to see what direction they can point me in, but the bottom line is that I have to live my life, not theirs.

How can we tell if a revealer is actually revealing a path that would be beneficial for us to follow? (If someone who makes allegations is an "alligator," is someone who makes revelations a "reveler"?) How long does someone follow a revealer? I have a friend, also an ex-Christian Brother, who went to Japan to a Buddhist monastery for about five years after he left the Brothers. He came back and seemed like a lost soul. In fact I heard that he became really unbalanced and he periodically runs naked and screaming in the streets. This is a sad and unusual example, but how long does one try to follow the teachings of others, or search for the great teacher?

The difficulty with searching for or following some great leader, or the followers of the followers of some great leader, is compounded by the fact that none of us is an objective searcher. If we were, 10 percent of the people born Catholic would remain Catholic, 10 percent would become Muslims, 10 percent Taoists, 10 percent Jews, and so on. Likewise, 10 percent of Baptists would become Buddhist, 10 percent Episcopalians, so on. But that's not the way it happens. Most religious believers are trapped by their beliefs, and really don't have the freedom to re-evaluate them. They find it impossible to say that one religion is as good as another if it serves your life.

Now I am going to reveal everybody's dirty little secret. Even though we claim to follow a particular religious leader, we don't. We follow our <u>own</u> insights, judgments, experience. In my own life, I thought that I was a follower of Jesus for many years. The truth is, I accepted some of what it is said that Jesus said, but I didn't accept other things. In fact virtually every Christian does this. The evidence is simple: how many one-eyed, one-handed Christians do you see walking around? And yet, didn't Jesus say, "if your eye scandalizes you, pluck it out; if your hand scandalizes you, cut it off." We should see piles of hands and eyes around the streets! Hold on, you say. He was speaking metaphorically (or whatever other explanation one comes up with). But by the very fact that you interpret what he said, you admit that you bring your own judgment to it. You are the arbiter, the judge. You follow your own experience and judgment, not Jesus'. You place what you say above what he says. In truth then, we disregard many things that our great spiritual leaders, or church, or our parents say. Yet we pretend that we are following teachings of these leaders, etc. That is our dirty little secret – or wonderful reality, once we come to admit it.

In this light, I was just thinking about what's called the Lord's Prayer, the Our Father. I had always revered this prayer, but the other day I got annoyed with it. I was thinking of the phrase, "lead us not into temptation." What kind of perverse god would lead someone into temptation? It would have to be a psychotic person who wants us to do good but tries to get us to do evil just to test us. So we have to plead with this person, "please don't lead me into doing evil, because I want to do good as you say. Lead me not into temptation." What a stupid phrase! Yet for many, many years I and millions of others have glossed over the phrase, pretended it wasn't there, just as we neglected to cut off our hands or pluck out our eyes. We say the Our Father is a beautiful prayer and pretend that parts of it aren't really dumb. So, even though we say we follow what great leaders have revealed, or what our church says they have revealed, we are really following our own counsel, belief or judgment.

How does one know, then, whom to follow (other than your own counsel)? Jesus had the best thing to say about this: "by their fruits shall you know them." Does he live in a way that is good, whole, integrated, joyful? If you're looking for a leader, look for someone whose life you admire. Look for someone who demonstrates your highest values. Let's change the paradigm for what "a leader" is. Don't look for someone who says, "follow me and trust me." Consider a leader as a pointer, someone who is pointing you in a direction: "here is the way I have come; examine whether this might be the way you want to go." (This is in no way a reflection on the Pointer Sisters.) We have to create our own path, but we test the direction they point to. Unfortunately, I think that most religious followers end up looking only at their interpretation of the pointer, and not what they are pointing to.

This leads me to a better interpretation of revelation, a more natural way of defining it. That is, revelation happens to all of us constantly. Everything we have in life is a gift – the sun, water, our lungs, our heart. When you think about it, even our thoughts are a gift. We don't do anything to create our thoughts; they just come to us. Every thought is a gift. Every thought is a revelation. But isn't there a difference between everyday thoughts and "inspired" thoughts? There is, but it's a qualitative difference. This is the continuum: thoughts, ideas, good ideas, great ideas, inspired divine ideas. The word "inspired" means "breathed into." Every thought is breathed into us, but some of them seem so good that we think that a god must have breathed them into us. We were inspired, revealed to. In this sense I do believe in revelation.

Summary

Revelation happens in a natural way, which is available to all of us. When people claim that they are special spokespersons for god, be wary: judge them on how they act. Also be wary of traditions passed on by your church or parents. Most people stick to the religious traditions they were brought up with, and not many come to realize the relativity of their beliefs. When they do, they see that revelation, especially about the meaning of existence, is something we can all have revealed to us naturally.

Chapter 7:

RELIGION

What is religion?

Religion is a story people make up to explain the universe we live in. More precisely, it is a story that one or a few people made up, and that many others accept, and embellish as they pass it on. The word "story" is not a negative word. As we saw earlier, everything we know about the world is an interpretation of what we experience. That interpretation is called a belief or story, which is what all the world' s religions are.

It is not a question of whether we need religion or not. It's a question of being here in the universe and trying to find some meaning to our presence here. Ultimately, we are trying to answer the question: Why do we exist? Why do I exist?

The way I have just described religion leads to the question of the difference between religion and philosophy. Most religions, in trying to explain the universe, come up with the idea of "god." Do you have to bring in god to explain the universe? I dedicate two chapters to this, so I will postpone answering this question. But, to take the question "Why do I exist?" a little deeper, let's look at why we ask "why"?

There are three ways of answering the question "why do we ask why?" The first is that it helps us to see the interrelationship of things. It is really a way of asking "how" – how things function together. For example, look at this series of questions:

- Why do plants flower? So they can germinate and bear fruit.
- Why do they bear fruit? So that they can repro duce themselves and that other creatures can eat the fruit.
- Why do plants reproduce themselves? So their life line can continue.
- And so on.

In this scenario the question "why?" really answers the question "how?" The answers we come up with show how things interrelate, how the parts of the universe function interdependently.

The second way to look at why we ask why is to ask what motivates someone to do something. E.g., "Why did you come home late?" When asking that question we may be looking simply for the "how" – what is the sequence of events that resulted in your being late? But often we mean it not as a question but as a statement: "This is not consistent with my expectations (**and** I am annoyed)" or "This is not consistent with how you generally operate." In either case, the answer still gives a "how." "Yes, here is the sequence of how I came to be late, and your annoyance is justified (or is **not** justified)" or "Here is the sequence of events, and here is how it does (or doesn't) fit in with how I generally operate." So, on this second level, the level of human motivation, the question "why?" still means "how?"

Then, of course, we come to the third way to interpret "why," the Big "why" question: why does the entire universe exist? When you are talking on this broadest scale, the question really means, "why do we exist rather than not?" I talk about this in the chapters on **God** and **The Meaning of Life**. But now I will come right out and give you my answer to the question, "why do we, the universe, exist rather than not?" The answer is: we just do! There may be another answer to that question that relates the universe to something else that we don't know about. But since we don't know about it and can't know about it, then according to my First Principal, it really doesn't matter. Even if there were an outside purpose, whatever it is doesn't negate that the fact that the universe, including us, is here, and it functions the way it does.

When you come to the level of being, the question why something is so simply helps you to realize more profoundly that it <u>is</u> so. For example, philosophers talk about "the intuition of being." When people focus on the question, "why do I exist?" or "why do I exist rather than not?" we come to realize or intuit the fact that we <u>are</u>, that we <u>do</u> exist. Experiencing our existence is the important thing, and asking "why?" just helps to experience it. Asking this question leads us to realize not only that we are, but also to experience the wonder, the awe, the damn good luck (grace) of having a chance to play on this stage. So, ultimately the purpose of religion is to experience, acknowledge and celebrate our existence, our being.

There seems to be a problem, however, with all religions. And that is that the story or myth which points to reality actually becomes the reality. Then we put all of our energy into preserving the myth, and we lose sight of the reality religion was meant to point to. The fundamental rule of most religions seems to be to love one another. Yet, as I write this, Muslims and Jews are killing each other in the Mideast, Catholics and Protestants in Northern Ireland, Croats and Serbs in the former Yugoslavia, Sikhs and Hindus in India and so on. As Jonathan Swift cleverly points out in *Gulliver's Travels*, the Lilliputians are fighting their enemy over the question of which end you should crack your egg on. The Big-endians claimed that they were right, and the Little-endians claimed that they were right. However, if you went back to be written source of their religion, their "Bible," it said that the egg should be broken "on the appropriate end." It's easy to lose sight of the fundamentals that the story points to and subscribe only to the story.

Given that this is so, we ought not to take religion so seriously. Lighten up! One story is as good as another as long as it serves life. The word "tolerance" summarizes it. We need to use religion to enable us to experience and live life. When the story does not fit what we experience, give up the story and make up another one. It is not religion, but our own experience, which guides us through life. A phrase I like that describes doing this is "the courage to be." It takes courage to base our lives on our own experience and to be willing to question the stories we have grown up with, or which other people approach us with, in order to reaffirm them or to supplant them with stories which better explain our over-all experience.

Summary

Religion is a story we make up to answer the question, "why do we exist?" Various religions have come up with different myths or stories that tell how we came to be and why we are here. They are all valid inasmuch as they point to the magnificent gift that it is to be, to exist. The problem with religion is that people cling to the stories and forget about the reality that those stories are meant to point out. Ironically, instead of being a source of harmony, religion then becomes a source of disharmony among people. Although I have only studied one religion in depth, I suspect that all religions point to a few basic truths: we exist, the universe is good, life is good, we didn't create all of this, enjoy it, be good to others, be forgiving. In short, enjoy your ride on the abundance train and help others to do so too.

Chapter 8:

CHURCHES

What is a church? Do we need them? What do I want from a church?

Back when I was in the Brothers, I was talking to Bro. Arthur Walsh about his friend. He asked his friend, "Why do you still go to church, given the many things you don't agree with?" His answer was, "What else do we have?" I think this reflects the feelings of many church-goers: "Yes, I get some value, but church is certainly not a source of profound vitality and spirituality for me." A lot of people are in a constant search for "a better church." It reminds me of how a Victorian described Unitarianism, "a featherbed to catch a falling Christian." ("I want <u>something</u>; maybe this will be better.") I don't mean to single out Unitarianism, but I love the quote. Some people do church-hopping: "Yes, I get some value here, but . . . ." When does the search stop? Is there a perfect church? Do I succumb and settle rather than select: "What else do we have?" Or do I get tired, drop the whole search and forget about church altogether?

If we start with the traditional definition of a church as a community of religious believers we are already in trouble. What's really there is a bunch of people who share similar religious beliefs. You would be hard pressed to find very many individuals who shared all of the same beliefs, even in the tightest knit group, once you scratched the surface and asked them what they meant by "I believe in such and such." It would be interesting to get groups of believers who call themselves "a church" and to have them list the 5 or 13 essential beliefs they held, and the next 5 or 13 secondary beliefs, and then to have them compare lists. In fact, that is what happened in the Reformation. Groups, mostly following a strong religious leader, or a strong secular leader whom they had no option not to follow, said, "These are the essential beliefs." Others said, "No, <u>these</u> are the essential beliefs." The history of the Christian churches since then has been one of splintering. As far as I can see, the Christian churches have divided mankind more than unified us. Now, that is not necessarily bad; in fact, according to my theory, it is good. People create new churches when they find that the beliefs and activities of the old one don't serve their life. Unfortunately, however, members of different churches or religions often tend to kill each other.

Why is this so? My guess is that they identify their belief with their being: if you challenge my beliefs, you are challenging me, my very existence. So, I better kill you in self-defense. On a deeper level, I suspect that religious conflict is really economic conflict at core. People use the religious trappings as an excuse to suppress and control others. Regardless, if people understood religious belief as a story we make up and choose to accept, then we wouldn't be so attached to our religion. We would be able to say: "Hey, here's the story I am making up. What story are you making up?" rather than, "Hey, you don't like my story; I'll kill you." As I said above, it is actually good to be divided on our beliefs, to have a variety of explanations of what's so – <u>if</u> it leads us to share them and to grow in vitality. But once we hold beliefs as absolute, we cut off life.

You also have to step back and follow the money. Who benefits from religions staying separate, rather than uniting? Who would be threatened by the statement that one church or religion is as good as another? Who would be threatened by the thought: "If this church doesn't help you grow, by all means go out and find another. After all, we only accept these beliefs because they are useful to us. If they're not useful to you, go out and find or create a group that share beliefs that empower you." What if the livelihood of pastors or rabbis or other religious leaders didn't depend on contributions from members of their congregation? Just a thought.

My main criterion for a church is: Does it help people grow personally/spiritually? (I find it difficult to distinguish between "personal" and "spiritual;" more on this later.) Churches exist only to facilitate people's growth, not vice versa. A church should be a vehicle to allow people to grow in their own direction. So, if they grow "out of" a church, or if they're "enduring" a lot in their church, it means the church is too wedded to its myth and is losing the reality of serving the spiritual/personal growth of individuals.

But wait a minute! Aren't churches meant to serve god, not man? I don't think so. We're in about the 12 billionth year since the Big Bang, on a $4\frac{1}{2}$ billion year old planet, the result of a 4th or 5th generation sun, with life showing up $3\frac{1}{2}$ billion years ago, and humans a quarter of a million years ago. Would the guy who made this, if there were one, get upset if we don't slaughter a lamb for him every Sunday? Religion and churches exist for man's benefit, not god's. God is sitting up there smoking a cigar watching the cosmic big bang oscillation series! There may be a purpose to worship (and it would be very useful to define just what is meant by "worship"), but that use or purpose serves man, not god. Even if you defined worship loosely as "a reminder of our creaturehood," does that reminder serve the needs of the creator or the created? All of this, of course, presumes a god, a creator. But if there were such a being, would he or she need to be thanked or acknowledged? I don't think so. On the other hand, I think it might be very useful for us to get together periodically to look at and be thankful for our existence.

Why Do Churches Persist?

So, why do churches persist, if they don't foster profound growth? What is it that makes them endure? Obviously they serve the needs of many people. Yet I think church communities often fulfill not the professed purpose of the church but other human needs. In looking at what needs churches fulfill, I came up with eight personal and four social values or benefits that churches seem to offer. The personal values are what a church can do for the individual, and the social values are what it can do for society.

The personal values are:

> 1. Safety/Security
> 2. Self-validation
> 3. Prayer/Reflection
> 4. Second Chance
> 5. Mutual Support
> 6. Ritual
> 7. Theater
> 8. Pastors' Pocketbooks

Here are the social values:

> 1. Community
> 2. Social/Good Works
> 3. Morality
> 4. Spiritual partying

These values, by the way, are all available in non-church or secular institutions as well, which I will point out. A "church" is not needed for any of them.

Personal Values

1. First, the value of **safety/security** can be expressed as: "I'm not alone in the world; life makes sense; death is O.K. too; I'm gonna make it. In fact, I did make it. All of us here are in the same boat, and it is good." If church gives us this value of safety/security, that's great. However, psychology and even education at its best can give us this value.

2. **Self-validation** ties in with number 1 above. "Chosen people" or redemption-oriented religions give people

the feeling: "We're O.K.; I'm O.K." Self-affirmation or self-validation are extremely important. Being chosen or redeemed was probably important way back when, when people did not have physical security, when other tribes or nations could overrun you and when the individual got his validation from being part of a group. But now we can get validation individually from psychology, education, family, or from taking a good long look at ourselves. The bottom line is that if you're here, you are automatically "god's chosen people." The universe voted on your validity by putting you here. It invested millions of years of chemical, genetic and social evolution to get you here the way you are. Your genes won the genetic game. You have a place in the universe because you have a place in the universe.

3. The next value is **prayer and/or reflection**. Going to church forces people into doing this, at least for a little while, every week. The real problem is that people just don't take the time to be with themselves and reflect on their own. You don't need church for this; you could just have the courage to take time to be with yourself regularly. Non-denominational prayer meditation groups exist as well. In addition, the ritual part of services often overwhelms the prayer part. See the chapter on **Prayer** for further discussion.

4. Next, church can give you a **second chance**. It gives you the vehicle to "repent," to let go of former ways of acting. At any moment we can re-possess our life and create a totally new now. Churches call it repentance or contrition, and on a bigger scale, being reborn. But even without churches we can recognize that something we did, or a way of being in the past, didn't serve others or ourselves. We can clean up the past, forgive ourselves, (ask forgiveness from others) and create a new future. There are a multitude of 12 Step groups, the most popular being Alcoholics Anonymous, that also help you do this. See the chapters on **Good and Evil**, and **Love and Morality**.

5. Churches give **mutual support** It's nice to be with a group of people who dress nice and aren't looking for a fight and who might even be benevolent and whom you can talk to. In addition, they might be inclined and able to help you. A folk-singing club could also do this (except the "dress nice" part). Any karass or granfaloon could do this. (Read Kurt Vonnegut's *Cat's Cradle*.) Or, look for a parenting group, a book club, or a hundred other affinity groups.

6. Church provides **ritual**. As I said before, god isn't too attached to slaughtered lambs, incense or advent wreathes. But these might do something for us. For one thing, some people like the consistency of doing the same thing in the same way. Did you ever try to show a two-year old a "better" way to do something? Forget it. You destroy their ritual; they destroy your peace of mind in return. Also, there is beauty in some of the ritual – sometimes hard to distinguish from pageant, pomp and circumstance – which some people like. Yet, we can have secular rituals as well; for example, a Japanese tea ceremony. Whatever your cup!

7. Looking at church as a source of **theater** ties in with number 6. As a matter of fact the Christian church was the source of the resurgence of theater in the middle ages. People would act out little liturgical scenes. The first, as I remember, was the "Quem queritis?" trope, the "Whom do you seek?" reenactment of the first Easter morning. Song and music followed. A large portion of the body of classical music is religious music. However, theater and music grew far beyond the boundaries of the church. (Is the theater legitimate, really?) So, we don't need churches now because we can go to plays and concerts. However, churches are a lot cheaper.

8. Church helps fill the **pastor's pocketbook**, or at least their stomachs. I had to slip in a little barb here. I suspect churches are like any other institution or bureaucracy. Those who run them and make their livelihood

from them have a vested interest in their continuance – whether or not they are actually accomplishing their original mission. I don't want to be too hard on church leaders. Actually, most pastors don't make as much money as they should. They should consider becoming secular preachers and make a lot of money by giving motivational seminars, showing people how to walk on hot coals and such! (If the shoe fits, wear it!) Here is where a lot of Protestant churches are better than the Catholics. It is the congregation who decides whether the shoe (Pastor) fits, not the Roman shoe manufacturer. (Damn, it feels good to get these little barbs out!) But this criticism can be leveled against all institutions – church, government, education – there are a lot of good people trapped in systems or bureaucracies that don't work, or work with gross inefficiency.

Social Values

Let's move to the social values that churches provide.

1. The first one, **community**, is a broad one. We can look at it both negatively or positively. Looking at it negatively first, people can band together as a community and become very insular, cut themselves off from the broader community and do very bad things – like the mass suicides of Heavenly Gate, Jim Jones in Guyana or David Koresh in Waco. (That poor town's name had two strikes against it to begin with!) Also, they could become a community of the persecuted, the downtrodden or the poor and validate how Karl Marx described religion: "The opiate of the people."

    Looking at community positively, a church can recognize and take care of each other's needs. It is comforting to be part of a group that gives you identity, especially within a larger and perhaps hostile environment. For example, Irish, Italian and other immigrants felt a sense of belonging and solidarity in the U.S. through the Catholic church. Latin Americans are doing likewise now against tyrannical rulers. Some are even rising up using the "Theology of Liberation" as their strength. Then again, there are secular groups that can provide these functions as well as a church: Solidarity, labor unions, the Italian-American Society, the Lions, Elks, the Jets and Sharks, the Crips and so on. Membership in these groups is good when it is a stepping stone for members to throw off literal and figurative victimhood, and to benefit from and contribute to the broader human community – which would eliminate a few I just mentioned.

2. A church that is carrying out **social/good works** is the broader sense of "community," the reaching out to the less fortunate in the human community. Carrying out good works has been one of the key validations and shining lights of churches: Soup kitchens, medical missionaries, Mother Theresa's work and all of the movements that reach out to the poor and those in need. Churches provide a structure for service and good works. You can always count on the churches! Even though an underlying motive has been and may still be to proselytize, many servants of the poor do it simply by their example, by service. I also remember Bro. Vincent Conti telling me, "If you give a hungry person a piece of bread, he doesn't care about your motives." However, secular groups, the Medecins Sans Frontieres, the Children's Defense Fund and others do the same thing.

3. Churches have been known to be great sources of **morality** – and also great sources of man's inhumanity to man as well, for god's sake! Churches have no monopoly on morality or immorality. Being a member of the human race without religion gives you just as good odds of being a moral person as being a church member does. I further discuss this in the chapter on **Love and Morality**.

4. Finally, churches are good for "**spiritual partying**." It depends what church you go to. Some people like the sense of theater they get from their church. They like

the pomp and circumstance, the ritual, the music that services provide. Other churches get people physically involved in singing, dancing and having an emotionally good time. Services can be a blast and a real high. An LSD party may yield the same result. Or just a regular party, or the Sweet Adelines. Or deep breathing.

That's my list of values that churches can provide to people. Churches clearly do provide spiritual value to many of their members. However, I suggest that many people remain in churches for the secondary values they provide, the personal and social values I have just outlined. It is fine to be in a church for these secondary values, but these in themselves are not the ultimate purpose of what a church is about. We need to be clear about the values our church gives to us, and to admit that this particular church is not necessarily the only vehicle for doing so. As my eighth grade teacher Sister Aurilla (probably one of my best teachers, and an early "fluke" – one who "goes back into the world" from the religious life) taught us in an old spiritual: "The ladder doesn't matter; it's the way that you climb. And we'll all get to heaven at the very same time." (With an attitude like that, they probably threw her out of the Sisterhood!) Churches give people value, if they give people value! Yet, all of the values churches provide can be obtained elsewhere.

As I said about religion, one church is as good as another, if it provides value. But that's not how churches usually think of themselves. They defensively claim, "We're the best!" True religion, true churches are inclusive, not exclusive. Given that definition, the only true church has a place for all belief systems. It is the one we call "humanity."

Could there be a church for all of humanity? This is quite a challenge, but I have taken some time to think about how such a church might be structured. We need some kind of "structure for fulfillment" for humanity to become all that we were meant to be. The purpose of a church should be to create a world that works for everyone. That implies a structure that supports both inward and outward growth:

it supports each individual to pursue their own spiritual and personal growth and it supports us together to heal and fulfill the planet. I have outlined some thoughts about such a church in Section 6 **A Church for the Millenium**.

Summary

The purpose of churches is to serve human needs, not to serve a god, if there is one - who has no needs. Churches are useful inasmuch as they do this, and not useful to the degree that they don't. All of the needs churches fulfill – most of which I have just outlined – can be served by other institutions as well. We need to be clear about what values we are looking for in a church, and the values our church provides. The law of natural selection will eventually win. A "true" church is inclusive, not exclusive. Given that definition, the only true church is one which includes all belief systems. It is called "humanity."

Section 3:

ABOUT THE EXISTENCE AND NATURE OF GOD:

Chapter 9:

GOD –
GOD AS A BEING

Does god exist?

I am finally ready to examine the big question and to answer it: Does god exist? To answer that question, let's first look at a few other questions which might help to illuminate this one. They are: Do refrinterals imply that we end after death, or that we go to a whole new, happier world? Are refrinterals benevolent or malevolent or neutral? Can refrinterals be reduced to one grand, unified concept, or do they necessarily have to be a plurality? Perhaps, the ultimate question is, do refrinterals even exist?

I hope that by now the question is growing in your mind, perhaps accompanied by some annoyance, "What the hell are refrinterals? Where did you come up with such a word?" If so, you are putting your finger on one of the fundamental questions in the universe. Here's why: There isn't any difference between asking whether refrinterals exists or whether god exists. The only difference between these questions is that we have been bandying the word "god" about for centuries, so everybody thinks they know what the word means. Whereas, refrinterals is a word I just invented, so it seems very obvious to us to ask what it means. Just as I invented this word, somebody invented the word "god." So we must ask of anyone who uses the word, "What does the word 'god' mean to you? Where did you come up with that word?" We presume that since we've been using the word so long, we know what it means, what it points to. This works on two levels. First, the human race has been using it for so long that surely, we, somebody, must know what it means! Secondly, I have been using it so long that surely I know what I am talking about! Let's challenge these two assumptions.

Further, asking the question begs the question. Asking whether something exists presumes its existence. When a word is commonly used and you ask if it exists, the question seems ridiculous. For example, if you ask, "do trees exist?" people will look at you a little strangely. Everybody knows what you mean by trees. But if you say, "do refrinterals exist?" you can't have any intelligent discussion until you say what you mean by that word. The trouble with the word "god" is that it is as common as the word "trees." Since it is so common, the instinctive reaction people have is, "everybody knows what 'god' means." Yet, as with all fundamental concepts, value comes from questioning the concept itself. That's why I spent so much time talking about truth and faith. True learning comes in questioning what is most basic, most elementary, most taken for granted. Asking a question like this, though, is threatening to people if they have never dealt with it before. To question is often perceived as negative – you are challenging, discounting or opposing something, and, by inference, the person you are questioning. Questioning doesn't necessarily have to do this, but when you keep asking, "Why do you say this? What do you mean by this?" people take it personally. Remember Socrates. A more fruitful way to look at questioning is that it will either get you more fully into the belief or more fully out of it. In other words, it will help you experience the reality behind the belief more fully, or will help you discard the belief if it is no longer useful.

So, does god exist? Tell me what you mean by the word "god," and I will tell you if god exists. Fundamental as the question "What do you mean by god?" is, it leads us to a second, even more fundamental question that I mentioned earlier: why is this belief important to you? What difference does it make whether there is a god, or a concept of god, or not? I don't ask this in a cavalier way, as if I were simply making the statement, "It doesn't make any difference whether god exists or not." I am asking you, as I have asked myself, what difference it would make. What would be lost to me if I didn't hold this belief? This question helps us to get to the fundamental values that we attach to this belief. It is the fundamental values that make the difference, not the belief they are attached to. Fundamentalist believers are not able to make this distinction. For them, the belief and value are one and the same. However, since I have written this primarily for myself and secondarily for the non-believer or fallen-away, we have the freedom to explore.

The Three Underlying "Needs" for a God

The fundamental question is: what difference does it make whether "god exists," or not? Why is the belief in god important to you? Here is my answer: It seems that historically "god" answers to our need for **meaning**: What's it all about – life, me, the universe? If there is no god, there is no meaning.

This search for meaning, as I see it, can be broken down into three big needs, three big questions people have had through the ages and that we still have today. They are:

- Where did the universe come from? And where is it going? Where did I come from? Somebody had to make all this. The underlying value is that we need a sense of order or a plan for the universe, not just randomness. We need a creator and care-taker.
- How can life be meaningful if we die? We are worried about death; how can life have any meaning if death is the end, period? Life wouldn't make sense if there were no god. If we just showed up here and then died, life would make no sense. We need a savior to save us from death by managing a world here-after.
- How are we to act in the world? People would just do whatever they wanted if there were no divine ruler. We

want a source for morality, a given code for how we should conduct our lives, especially how we should act toward each other. We need a lawgiver who is also a judge and can punish people for harming others.

Let's put labels on these concepts. "God" seems to be necessary for:

A. **Creation** – Where did we come from? (How did we get here?)
B. **Mortality** – What happens after death? (Where are we going?)
C. **Morality** – How should we act? (What do we do while we're here?)

I will come back to explore what these three concepts mean, and whether they are sufficient rationale for positing a god. Before I do that, let me make a distinction between **a** god, and other possible ways of looking at god. **A** god means that a distinct being exists out there. This is what most people who speak of god have in mind. However, it seems to me that there are five possibilities of what people can mean by the word "god." God could be:

1. <u>a</u> being
2. <u>in</u> beings - a spirit
3. being
4. <u>all</u> beings
5. a metaphor

My adding the last one, god as metaphor, tips my hand as to the direction my thinking has taken me. In this chapter I will discuss #1, god as <u>a</u> being. In the next chapter I will discuss the other 4 possibilities. It is god as <u>a</u> being that seems to answer the three needs I just discussed.

1) God as <u>a</u> Being

First, let's look at the possibility of god existing as <u>a</u> being. My life has shifted from a strong belief that this was so, to a strong belief that this is quite impossible. Yet, I would guess that this is the image that most people in the Judeo-Christian tradition still have of "god"—a kind (or wrathful), bearded, old man paternally taking care of the universe. Part of the problem is that in order to create an image, you necessarily <u>have to</u> use <u>a</u> being (or beings) to do it. You can't picture something invisible. Why did people come up with this fatherly image of god (or motherly as many ancient religions had)? Let us get back to the three fundamental questions I just described. The needs give rise to the three different ways we see god as <u>a</u> being. God is:

- creator and caretaker of the world
- "savior" of the world, especially one who saves us after death
- lawgiver and judge of the world.

Let's look further at these concepts.

A) Creation - Where Did We Come From?

If the universe didn't exist, would there be a god? That is an interesting question. It sort of takes the wind out of our sails. If there weren't any universe, who cares whether there is a god or not? It would be a stupid academic debate – which begs the question, since there would be no debaters around. So, just wrestling with this question, makes me realize that the overriding reason we have come up with the theory of a god is to explain or understand the universe we are part of.

This is a very fundamental question: How in the world did we show up here? Where did we all come from? What's the source of me, of us, of the universe? There must be some source, some creator of the universe – let's call him "god." This is what most people would say they mean by god — creator of the universe. The next question is: what do you mean by "creator of the universe?"

To answer that question we will first have to engage in the "great belly button debate." We have to look at whether the creator or source of the universe is an "innie" or an "outie" – like the two styles of belly buttons. The question then is, is there a source of the universe within the universe itself, an "innie" god, or is the source outside of and separate from the universe as we know it, an "outie" god?

Let's start with the "innie" theory (and make short shrift of it). Could we say that a god, a creator or source of the universe, is within the universe? The question immediately comes up, "if so, where?" Where would she be, on Pluto? How would a Plutonian be directing everything else? When we phrase the question in this way, the reason we can't have an innie god is apparent. A part couldn't have created the whole, and then manage the whole. How can a being who is a part of being be the source of all being? It is self-contradictory to say there is a god in the universe, an innie god.

Most current western theology seems to be based on the outie theory of god. At first glance, it seems like a pretty reasonable theory. It seems that something bigger, smarter than the universe should be its source. When you look at the vast, wonderful complexity of this evolving universe, you say: "God, somebody very smart and powerful – in fact, infinitely wise, loving and omnipotent – must have made this place." Greater can't come from less. For example, a rock can't produce a tree. If we see our own ability to know and love and do as the highest powers in the universe, it seems that our source would be a better knower, lover, doer – a bigger person – than we are. It takes a big person to make a universe! Such a powerful being can't be in the universe; he has to be outside of it. In short, the universe must have been out-sourced, so to speak, and god an "outie" god.

Although this is plausible, we could just as easily make a case for greater coming from less, since "higher" life forms (that's us) have evolved from "lower" life forms (lizardoids, etc.). So maybe we're evolving toward creating god at the end of this whole process. Sort of like "slouching toward Bethlehem to be born." (This is a "literary reference." Don't worry if you don't get it.) Maybe this is why Christians are so jazzed about the "second coming of Jesus." (Another literary reference.) It reflects the forward thrust of evolution. As a matter of fact, trees <u>did</u> come from rocks. It just takes a little time for the swirling matter of the universe to evolve into stars and planets and rocks and then into trees.

Here is the problem with the outie theory of god. If a god exists outside of and distinct from the universe, then he/she/it, by definition, can't be known by us. We can only know things within the universe, within the realm of our own experience. We can't know what is outside of our power to know. It's like being able to speak Mongolian without having ever been to Mongolia or heard or read the language. That's why very smart theologians say that god is "ineffable." "Ineffable" literally means "not able to be spoken about."(This doesn't prevent them, of course, from doing a lot of speaking anyhow!) You can't know about what you can't know about. We are stuck inside the universe, so that's all we can know about. If we can't know about an outie god, there is nothing we can say about her.

Part of the reason this seems so is from our use of the word "creator." When we say "creator" we mean somebody who makes something out of something. To make something, we take something else and reshape or combine it. There are always raw materials that are acted upon. We ask, where did the raw materials come from? From other raw materials. And where did they come from? And so on. In our experience, creation always comes out of something preceding it. We make up the saying that god is "the uncaused cause" or uncreated creator of the universe, but we have no way of conceiving that. It is entirely out of our ability to know, since we only know "caused causes," such as a cake is caused by its ingredients, its baker and so on.

In addition, cause and effect always take place in time. A seed grows into a tree. I cut the tree down and make a bench from the wood. Or, on the most personal level, I exist first, then I have children, then they have children and so on. The problem is that we are taking an anthropomorphic view of the universe, one with a beginning, middle, end – because that's what our lives look like. We are born, we live, we die. So we think, "Who began all this? Who fired off the big bang?" There is, though, a different way to understand time.

Briefly, time is simply a measure of change. A year means the earth circled around the sun once. To die at 80 means the earth orbited the sun 80 times between your birth and death. But then, the sun will die some day too. Perhaps this expansionary phase of the universe for the last 10 or 15 billion years will peter out, collapse, and then the universe will contract, have a "big implosion" and die. Or, maybe it will bang out again. So, time is just a measure of stuff happening in relation to other stuff. We're inside of a system of "stuff happening." So, maybe there is no "pre" or "post" to the universe. "Time" and "maker" are just ways we talk about things that don't and can't apply to the whole universe. If you say stuff happened which caused this stuff to happen, then the first "stuff" is just another part of the "stuff happening." A Big Time-maker would just be a part of stuff, and then be relegated to the status of a little time-maker like us.

The universe, by definition, encompasses everything. There is nothing outside of the universe to measure it against. So, the universe is outside of time. Universe-wise, there is just an ever-present now, with the universe busily doing a lot of neat things. Taking an outside-of-time view, we realize that we are part of an ever-changing cyclical show. The show didn't come to be but just is, and we are a tiny part whose atoms and cells and breath and knowing and interaction roll in and then roll out like all other parts of the show.

I am not saying that there couldn't be a being who exists outside of the universe, but, if so, she is entirely unknowable to us. This is where I invoke Sanitate's First Principle: If you can't know something, then it doesn't matter. We know that <u>we</u> are, that the universe is. Whether it was caused by a somebody doesn't add or detract from what is.

Another way of looking at the "outie" and "innie" question is to talk about intelligence in the universe. We can say that there must be intelligence <u>beyond</u> the universe, or there must be intelligence <u>within</u> the universe. Well, we clearly know that there is intelligence within the universe. All you have to do is open your eyes. If there is intelligence within the universe, does it make any difference if there is intelligence beyond it? No more than if there were intelligent life within the universe with whom we could never come into contact. When, however, you want to personify the possible intelligence outside of the universe and make it "Intelligence," my question is, "why?"

On the other hand, the more I wonder at the improbability of all of this, of this wonderful, universe evolving out of a big bang, and me a knowing part of it, the more I want to say, "This can't all be by accident; there must be something above, beyond all this, outside all of this. There must be an eternal god in charge." And yet I know that a "must be" doesn't equal an "is." It doesn't prove anything. Yet how could it not be? That thought just keeps recurring. Obviously, there is no answer. Or maybe better to say, there is no obvious answer. The answer is a belief, a choice. You either choose the "there must be" part, or you choose the "there must be doesn't mean there is" part. Or you choose the fact part: "nobody knows," or more accurately, "I don't know."

In summary, it seems that in the first case (innie) there can't be <u>a</u> god, and in the second case (outie) we can't know whether there is, and it is impossible to conceive of one. In the long run, however, it really doesn't make much difference. I know it just seems more comforting and reassuring if there were an outie god, a "big guy" out there, handling things – a nice, solid answer to our questions, "Where did we come from? Who's in charge here?" However, whatever you have to say about how we got here doesn't add or detract from the fact that we're here!

B) Mortality - What Happens After Death?

This brings us to a second reason that people say there is an outie god: People are afraid of dying. Death is probably the biggest gut-level reason people believe in an outie god. If there is a Bigger Person out there, then maybe there is a place for us to go when we die. Maybe something new and better happens to us after death (or something worse if we've been bad). We don't want this life to be "it" – the whole shebang, the whole enchilada, all there is. We hope there's somebody managing things out there so we can have a life after this one. The chapter, **Afterlife**, explores this topic. For now, I assert that if we didn't die, and we were omnivivacious (something like that), we wouldn't have any need to invent god. In fact, if we didn't die, people probably wouldn't spend two seconds worrying about a source of the universe. We would be immortals – we would be gods! But we aren't immortal, so we need somebody to save us after death.

Again, it seems more comforting and reassuring if there were a Big Momma out there who would make everything better when we die, but it just doesn't seem likely. (I bet you can't wait to get to the chapter on afterlife now!) We can't base this life on the hope of something in the future. We need to live life to the fullest now and not alter it based on something nobody knows anything about – that is, what happens after death. In fact, if I were a betting man, I would have to say, "Presume death is the end. Presume that what you see is what you get, so live life in a way that makes sense here and now."

During the history of the world when life has been difficult for most people, this life hasn't looked like a very good deal. In fact, when one fifth of the world is fighting hunger and malnutrition every day today, this life may not look like a good deal right now. Maybe the hope of an afterlife has gotten people through. Then again, maybe the world would have progressed more quickly if religion hadn't served as the opiate of the people. But very strongly wanting something to be so, like a god who manages an afterlife, doesn't necessarily make it is so. Since we can't know what happens after death, according to Sanitate's first principle, it doesn't matter.

C) Morality - How Should We Act?

The third big reason that people invent a god is that they think there would not be any morality or values without a god. It is god's law that determines what we value and how we act. If there were no afterlife and no god, wouldn't people just let loose and perpetrate all kinds of immoral acts? We need a Law-giver and a Judge for us to live moral lives. That is the argument.

In my chapter on **Love and Morality** I argue that morality derives from mankind's judgment of how to best live with each other. It is a result, like most other things, of natural selection. It is what works. The fittest way for mankind to survive is to not kill each other, steal from each other, etc. Suffice it to say for now that even if "god" had not said: "Thou shalt not kill," it is not such a good idea anyhow, and most people agree. If you kill somebody, their family will try to kill you and so on, and this doesn't make society work well. So morality really doesn't need the premise of a lawgiver god who will punish us for being bad.

Some are afraid that this philosophy would lead to an immoral "eat, drink and be merry" philosophy. When I step back to look at the "eat, drink and be merry philosophy," however, it sounds like one of the most moral philosophies I have ever heard! In fact, I'll go a step further and say that it is the source of morality. But that is only if we start with the premise that everybody needs to eat, drink and be merry. As a matter of fact, tomorrow we all do die! Would this philosophy lead to selfishness and hedonism? I doubt it. I bet the vast majority of readers of this book personally can not be merry if someone next to them is starving to death. If we look into our heart of hearts and get over our irrational fears, all we really want to do on this planet is to create a world of self-sufficiency where everybody can eat and drink, where no one dies of hunger or poverty. Then we can move on to maximizing the "merry" part, to explore how we can all have life and have it more abundantly. I long for the day when every developing world citizen can watch golf on TV, or better yet, play it – or to do their cultural equivalent.

Morality and mortality fit together for some people. It is reassuring to think of a god who laid down the law here and who will punish the people who were bad on earth after death. Morality is imposed from without, and reward and punishment will come after death, if it doesn't seem to be happening in this world. However, none of the three fundamental questions about the source of the universe, an after-life or morality show that there must be a god who exists as a being.

Summary

When speaking about whether "god" exists, we need to say what we mean by the word. The five ways in which people have thought about god are that god is:

1. a being
2. in being - a spirit
3. being
4. all beings
5. a metaphor

The concept of a god is an answer to the fundamental questions that mankind is always trying to answer:

A. Creation – Where did we come from?
       (How did we get here?)
B. Mortality – What happens after death?
       (Where are we going?)
C. Morality – How should we act?
       (What do we do while we're here?)

People seem to mean by "god" one or more of these three things:

- creator and caretaker of the universe
- savior of the world
- lawgiver and judge of world

In summary, all three of these concepts of god are stories we invented to make up answers to the fundamental questions about where we came from, why we die, and how we should act. They are a matter of faith, which help some people to fulfill the need to explain creation, death and morality. I suggest that there are better stories we can make up to understand these fundamental questions, or, to fulfill these fundamental needs. Finally, these three needs rely on a concept of god as a being, who, historically has been an outie being, someone outside of the universe, and therefore entirely outside of our capacity to know. Likewise, an innie god is implausible because how could someone who is part of something create that something?

To look at the majesty of the universe, and say there must be a god doesn't necessarily mean there is. It is hard to imagine a god who exists as a being. The next chapter looks at the other four possibilities.

Chapter 10:

GOD – OTHER POSSIBILITIES

I decided to break the "**God**" chapter in two for easier reading. In the last chapter I gave the five ways in which people have thought about god. To repeat, they are that god is:

1. a being
2. in being - a spirit
3. being
4. all beings
5. a metaphor

I discussed #1, god as a being, in the last chapter, so this brings us to #2. Perhaps we can revive the idea of an innie god, one who lives within the universe or in us. This, of necessity, means that god would have to be a spirit. Let's explore that concept.

2) God as *in* beings - *a spirit*

What about the possibility of god being not a being, but within being – a "spirit." If god were a spirit – something without a body or matter – that would eliminate the need to have him or her anywhere. God could be everywhere within the universe.

However, just what do we mean by "spirit"? Where did

that word come from? Getting back to the Latin root of the word, "spiritus" means "breath." Breath is that invisible thing, which is not really a thing but which is in all living beings. However, without getting into exactly what "material" means, breath could be considered as material. Although we cannot see it (except on cold days), we can feel it. So, what is the big deal about breath, or spirit? This: When we die our breath, the spirit, leaves us. If one has a very strong prejudice against dying, which includes most of the human race, one could say that although the body decays the breath or spirit goes on existing somewhere else. We dissociate the breath or spirit from the breather to make death acceptable. Once we give it an existence of its own, we can go on to theorize about things like "possession," where one spirit enters into the body of another. Or, on to re-incarnation where the spirit moves from a body that dies into a new one being born.

The problem with this is that in our experience of the universe – in my experience, anyhow – there aren't any "spirits," just "spirited beings." You never have spirit unless it is in some living being. You don't have any breath unless you have a breather. On a broader scale, you don't have motion, force or energy in the universe, unless you have something in motion – this implies distinct beings.

Then again, the new quantum physics says there really is no matter, no stuff, in the universe. There's nothing out there, no-thing, just energy fields, or "possibility amplitudes," as Deepak Chopra says. (Isn't that reassuring: nothing's the matter!) That may be, but it reminds me of Samuel Johnson's way of proving a rock's existence – by kicking it. Even if there is ultimately no-thing, the world still manifests itself as distinct, corporeal beings. All being has a be-er, one who "be's." You can't predicate being unless you have a subject who's "doing" the being, or who "be's."

We can even take a lesson from English grammar. Nouns are the doers, the subjects of sentences. Verbs are what they're doing – or being. For example, there is no such thing as "running." There is only, "John runs." "Running" or "being" are abstractions we make up. You can't have "being" without physicality, without somebody or something that is and that carries out the activity – not in the universe I live in anyhow.

To have a god that is _in_ being, then, doesn't make sense. What animates each being seems to be specific to that being. If god is in me, am I two people? Maybe a lot of spirits inhabit me. Who is the real me? Let's keep it simple. There is one breathing me, inhabited by only me. At my last breath, my "spiritus" is gone. It is carbon dioxide passing into the atmosphere, and then my body decomposes and passes into the earth and the atmosphere. To have a god that is _a_ spirit, or just spirit, seems an unnecessary and unlikely addition. O.K. then, what about a god that is just _being_ itself?

3) God as _being_

Perhaps god is just "being." But, similar to what I just said, it is hard to see how you can have just "is-ness," that is, "being," without somebody or something that is "doing" the being, somebody that be's. To have a god who is just "being" doesn't match anything within the realm of our experience. Once you call the verb "being" a noun, it seems you are necessarily talking about an outie god and therefore an unknowable one. To talk about being without be-ers, is something totally beyond my bounds of comprehension. It could be so, but I can't see it - literally or figuratively.

4) God as _all_ beings

If there is a god that is not "being" itself, perhaps all beings, everything is god; perhaps you and I and all of us and the whole universe is god! If the universe has no source outside of itself, perhaps it is its own source. This belief is commonly know as pantheism.

One drawback to this theory, perhaps, is that the universe is mortal. We came into existence 12 billion years ago, and we may pop out of existence in another 12 billion. Nobody knows. The next question is: if we are mortal, could we still be considered "god"? That leads us to challenge a basic assumption: why does god have to be immortal? What if god were just the sum total of the universe, and if and when it goes, god goes? If god is the entire universe, if the universe just "sources" itself, if it just is – mortal though it may be – then we all share in "godhead" to some degree. (How come we never talk about "devilhead," by the way?) Mankind says: "What a fine piece of luck – we just showed up! Isn't that divine! Aren't we divine!"

Yet, the question "Why?" keeps coming up. Why all of this? Why do we all exist rather than not? One time long ago in college I asked myself, "Why does god exist?" (You may be asking, "Did this young man have a lot of time on his hands, or what?"). The answer came to me, "because he just does; there is no 'reason.' God doesn't need a reason to be, he just is." From Aristotle's "Four causes" point of view, god is the final cause (reason or purpose), the uncaused cause. He has no reason or final purpose or end, other than that he just is. Then I thought, why don't we say the same thing about ourselves: We exist simply because we do! We are our own reason for being. We exist "just because," or, as my son Jamie said as a three year old, "Cause-be we do." I like that belief: we are our own reason for being. Inasmuch as god is an "uncaused cause," a being whose purpose is nothing other than to be, likewise for us, and for the entire universe, mortality notwithstanding.

That brings up the question, "If the whole universe passes out of existence, wouldn't our whole existence be meaningless?" My answer is a resounding "No." The universe, the earth and each individual are all wonderful, magnificent, all miracles in ourselves. Just look around and see what a blessing life is. And even though we all pass away, there is immeasurable possibility in us while we are here. So what if we all die? This is not a bad deal. Wake up and smell the roses (or coffee)! We get to invent, to make up the meaning of the universe. Another way of saying it is that we get to create the meaning or purpose of our own lives, and in an anthropomorphic sense, the meaning of the whole universe. The meaning we assign to life is the meaning of life. We can say that the purpose of life is to eat bread, look at sunsets, build houses, play with the kids, study anthropology, play golf, eliminate polio, end hunger, go to the movies . . . whatever we choose. That becomes the meaning of our life simply because we say so. However, I am jumping the gun here and will talk further about this in the **Meaning of Life** chapter.

Getting back to the possibility that god is <u>all</u> being, <u>is</u> the universe, then why not just eliminate the middle person? If creation is an internally generated, on-going phenomenon, we don't really need to have a "creator." Why do we have to bring in the concept of god at all? Why not just say that we, the universe, are? Is the concept of god passé? In one sense, yes. Just like Santa Claus, the concept was useful to us for a while, and I dare say still useful to many. Perhaps it is time for mankind's weaning (we have to stop being "weenies"!), so we can start taking responsibility for our divinity, for creating our share of the universe.

In another sense though, we need to evaluate the concept of god as we evaluate any other concept: How useful is it? What is the value behind it that we are affirming? When we look at other concepts like love or justice or integrity, even though they don't exist as things, they are still useful as concepts. So, the concept of god may still be useful as, what I call, "the Grand Metaphor."

5) God as the Grand Metaphor

In the final analysis, I believe the word "god" can be seen as the Grand Metaphor. (Final analysis means that this is the way I see it at this point.) A metaphor is a word or phrase that stands for something else because of a similarity between the two things. (For example, "You light up my life" does not mean "You set me on fire" – which is another metaphor in itself, come to think of it.)

What does this metaphor, god, stand for? It attests to the joy, wonder and awesomeness of existence, of life – of this freely-given (gratis – gratia – grace), ever-evolving piece of time/space in which we have the opportunity and privilege to have and to create our lives. I use the word "Grand" because the old concept of god is that of one who embodies all of our highest values: All-Knowing, Loving, Beautiful, Wise, Giving, Awesome, Glorious, Joyful and so on. These values attest to the "grandness" of life. We have the ability to know, to love, to experience beauty, and all the other marvels of life. The word "god" makes us step back and look at how wonderful life really is. So, maybe talking about god shakes us out of the tyranny of the urgent and mundane, so that we do, in fact, smell the roses of existence.

I am not sure if I have been too wordy or not wordy enough in the last paragraph. Here's what Barbara Marx Hubbard says about god: "God is understood as the co-creative intelligence running through the spiral of evolution, now becoming self-aware in us."

Let me say a word about "ever-evolving" nature, or, in the words I used earlier, "forward thrust" of the universe. We can look at the universe as ever-flowing, ever-enhancing energy – from the motion of particles, to the motion of atoms, to the interaction of molecules, to planetary and galaxial motion, to life, to human breath and consciousness, to thought and word, to love and inter-connection. All energy, all motion, is interrelated. So, maybe the use of the word "god" is similar to what physicists call the GUT, the Grand Unifying Theory. Physicists are searching for a theory that explains all movement, all energy, all the four forces in the universe in a unified way. The word "god" attests to the orderly motion, or forward thrust, or intelligent unified energy of the universe.

Perhaps we needed the idea of an outie god in the infancy of human knowledge, and the idea of an innie god, or Grand Metaphor, in the adolescent phase of our development. As we move into maturity as a human race we may simply acknowledge the sacredness of life and existence, and live as if it were so. One thought that has occurred to me is that if we acknowledged that "there ain't nobody here but us chickens" – that is, nothing here but us galaxies, stars, planets, living beings, people, etc. – then we would have to take responsibility for our "godliness." We would have to have the courage to be, to acknowledge that we <u>are</u>, that we share in being, or Being, or godhead. We get to be responsible to create our own lives, our own meaning in life. All of us to some degree are whiners and victims in life. It's easier to not take responsibility and not be godlike. We have great excuses, primarily pain and death. If I'm part god, why do I have to suffer? Why do I have to die? That's why Christianity has been such a potent force: "OK, wise guys, I <u>am</u> god, and I suffer and die, so stop bitching!"

A short word about pain and death – pain and death may be inevitable, but suffering is optional. We should sympathize with those in pain, just as we would want them to do for us – and even sympathize with those who create suffering out of their pain. But when it comes to personal pain, see what you can do to alleviate your pain, but always be responsible for creating your own life, which means, don't suffer. But I am getting ahead of myself again. See the chapter on **Good and Evil**.

Are we ready to be who we are, without the metaphor?

Several of the preceding thoughts are tied together by a wonderful concept Alan Watts came up with – the idea of "a bored god." If "god" knew everything already, he would get pretty bored! So, god created a game for himself whereby he is just as in the dark about the future as we are. This leads us to the realization that to know the future is a contradiction in terms. For example, if you knew you were going to be hit by a car while crossing a street today then you would just avoid crossing that street. And then you wouldn't be hit by the car. So you really didn't know the future! If we knew things would turn out badly, we would change them. So, de facto, we can't know the future.

This gives rise to the thought that god is a metaphor for the process of natural selection, where it is impossible to know what will happen. To give a better sense of the process, let's say that we knew the future, but there was no way we could change it. What if we were a rock, for example, that knew a steamroller was coming this afternoon to crush us? As humans we would avoid the steam roller; as a rock we have no locomotion. But, if we were a knowing rock, we would somehow create change so as to move ourselves. Knowing means being able to see how the universe operates, and that creates the possibility for us to use and benefit from that operation. How could a rock know a steam roller was coming? It would have to have an understanding of how motion works and would thus have a capacity to create the means to provide motion for itself. Not immediately, but in billions of years. It, we would, evolutionarily, develop legs and get out of the way. So, maybe this one rock won't be able to escape the steam roller, but intelligent rocks (that's us) gradually learn to change things, so that, today, not too many people get run over by a steam roller. If they did, it would be part of the process of natural selection – getting rid of stupid people who can't seem to get out of the way of steam rollers!

Even if there were an outie god, she would be a god embedded in the nature of the evolutionarily unfolding universe, one who has no idea of the outcome of atoms bumping up against each other to form molecules, or cars bumping up against each other to form a traffic jam, or humans bumping up against each other to end hunger and population growth on the planet (or conversely to destroy it). It's all up in the air. It's all up to us. Nothing is for sure. Isn't that great! Isn't that not boring? God is a golfer. If she knew she would shoot 70 every day, she wouldn't come out to the course! So, instead of saying god is embedded in the universe, we could say that god is the universe. That is, there is no distinction between the gloriously on-ward and up-ward thrust of this evolutionary universe and god. And it isn't onward and upward unless we make it so. It doesn't have to turn out that way. We are god. But then, why is there a need to posit a god at all? There isn't. So god is a glorious metaphor to enable us to recognize the marvelous magnificent unfolding of creation in which we are privileged to take a part. How improbable it is that I, we, exist in this magnificent play field! How grateful I am for this opportunity. Watts also says in *The Book*, p.70: "He (the individual) may be seen instead as one particular fo-

cal point at which the whole universe expresses itself . . . ."
What a charming idea, that we are not individuals but the
focal point of the universe. There is no center of the universe. Everything is relative to everything else. We are all
focal points, valid and real and living focal points, yet only
parts of the whole. In this sense as well, we are each god,
each the center-point part of this marvelous unfolding.

Then is it valid to speak about god at all? For now, yes. It is
a wonderful metaphor for helping us understand our humanness and divinity, our essence, and the nature of reality. It is a way of self-discovery, of speaking of ourselves.
As long as we know that we can't know anything about
an outie god and that when we speak about god, it is a
wonderful vehicle to helping us discover the nature of reality, then it is O.K. to go ahead and do it. For example,
you might say that if there were no god then we wouldn't
have to have respect for one another. Well, the important
thing is that we have respect for one another. If you need
the concept of god in order to have respect for one another, that is fine. Yet, realize it is the respect for one another that counts. Or let's say that if there were no god the
universe wouldn't make sense. The important thing is that
the universe makes sense. If the universe made sense to
someone without an outie god being in the picture, then
that is fine too. The grand metaphor allows us to get down
to fundamental values. If you can get to them without the
metaphor, that's even better.

In conclusion, I suggest that god is the Grand Metaphor
pointing to something very valuable to a lot of people over
the ages. To get to the value behind the use of the word,
we have to ask: What would it mean if there were no such
word? What would be lost? What is the value that the word
points to? The value is not so much a being, but a quality
of being: the intelligent, loving/gracious, beautiful, forward-thrusting energy/life force of/in atoms, stars, creatures, people, the universe. This is my current understanding and phrasing for the metaphor, "god." You can understand now why people use the word "god." Can you
imagine people singing the popular hymn: "Praise intelli-

gent, loving/gracious, beautiful, forward-thrusting energy/life force of/in atoms, stars, creatures, people, the universe from whom all blessings flow"?

Even if there were an outie god, a separate, all-powerful, all-knowing, etc. being, she lets us act on our own. She doesn't need us, she doesn't get upset if we don't worship her. We can't know her, so we can make up whatever stories we like – as I am doing here – and she won't get mad! She will forgive me if I am wrong!

A final caveat here. I remember my friend Cristiam saying, "Please don't do away with god yet in your book." The thoughts I share with you in this book come from me, from this specific focal point in the universe. Although I am being as "objective" as possible, I want to here try to "step outside of myself" to let you know who it is that is sharing these thoughts. I have had very few, if any, mystical experiences. I have tried to meditate a lot, but I don't consider myself successful at it. I very seldom have profound experiences, which could be interpreted as experiencing my higher self or "god." I am much more rational than emotional. What all this means is that maybe I am missing the boat about all this! Maybe there is that loving father or mother who is in charge, who will take care of things after death. This certainly is more attractive than "the Grand Metaphor"! And I wouldn't mind it one bit. There are many writers who have had mystical experiences, and who might balance what I have to say.

However, I have to be who I am, and I am compelled to call it the way I see it. I pride myself on integrity. (Integrity, by the way, is not something that one has; it is something which one has the opportunity to continue to get more and more of throughout life.) The thoughts I am sharing in this book are what I can say with integrity so far. I consider them an essential house-cleaning, an essential foundation for anything else to be built on. I love to be rational. Foundations have to be planned out, thought out, linear, rational. Maybe as I continue to grow in life, I will have more profound experiences. Maybe I will come to experience "god" in one of the first four senses I have just described, or in an entirely new way. I would welcome that. Maybe there will be a grand sequel to this book: Now that the house has been cleaned out, we can furnish it!

Summary

In this chapter, I look at the last four ways of the five ways in which people have thought about god:

1. <u>a</u> being
2. <u>in</u> being - a spirit
3. being
4. <u>all</u> beings
5. a metaphor

After looking at possibilities 1 through 4, I come to the conclusion that god is the Grand Metaphor, #5. Our use of the word "god" attests to the joy, wonder and awesomeness of existence, of life – of this freely-given (gratis – gratia – grace), ever-evolving piece of time/space in which we have the opportunity and privilege to have and to create our lives. All being is "godly" because we participate in the motion/energy/life force of the universe. To the extent that we share in being, we are all god. We get to create the meaning of life. This is not diminished by the fact that we all die, and that the universe may die as well.

The "Grand Metaphor" pulls us back and makes us reflect on this marvel of existence. The trick is to not abandon the reality for the metaphor. People spend their lives killing each other over metaphors. Metaphors are great as long as they help you to embrace the reality. That should be, by the way, the measure by which we evaluate the validity of the metaphor – to what degree does it help us embrace the reality. A shortened version of the reality that the Grand Metaphor "god" points to is that we are an intelligent, loving/gracious, beautiful, forward-thrusting energy/life force of/in atoms, stars, creatures, people, the universe. Rejoice!

Chapter 11:

AFTERLIFE

What happens after we die? Is there an afterlife?

Earlier I said that the main reason people believe in a god is that they hope for a life after death. Whether there is life after death no one knows. My friend Ron Hansell says that clearly there is an afterlife; it just may not involve the deceased! However, whether the deceased have an afterlife, we can only speculate. The evidence to me points to this life being total and complete in itself for each being, and when you're gone you're gone!

If we were to come back, it would either be on a physical or spiritual level. Let's look at both.

Do We Come Back Physically?

I can't conceptualize how we could exist in a physical way after death. The body decays after death. Does it get reconstituted? If so, where? If someplace, how do I get there? What age will I be when I come back? What will my body be composed of – living cells? If they are living, that means they will have to die again. They and we will have to be birthed, grow and die all over again – and again and again. It is unimaginable to have physicality like we have now unless we have a world just like the one we have right now. That means we'd have an endless cycle of births and deaths.

Perhaps that is what happens. Perhaps this is not my first

incarnation. Maybe this <u>is</u> the afterlife of another me who lived earlier! Maybe I died and went to heaven, and this is it! We're all in heaven right now! I bet you feel short-changed, right? This doesn't seem like a very good possibility, unless you posit that your parents came back just exactly as they were for you in this life, and all your environment came back exactly, and the whole universe came back exactly as it was when you first got here. How we came to be here and now is a composite of trillions upon trillions of events, and the you that's you now couldn't be you except for all those events having happened. But wait a minute. That's sort of self-centered, just looking at a return from your point of view. What about your parents? Your kids? How can you and your parents and kids come back as well? For them to come back, the whole world would have to be constituted as it was when <u>they</u> were born. In fact, if everybody came back, all of history would have to exactly repeat itself.

That gives rise to the old cosmic hiccup theory. That is, maybe the whole universe keeps repeating itself. The whole big bang birth and death process keeps repeating itself. Whether that is true or whether we are here only once and then gone, it wouldn't make a bit of difference, would it? We wouldn't know if this was our first reincarnation, or our 2,001st. We live our lives as if this were a one shot deal; we have no memory of past lives or knowledge of future ones. So, even if we existed before, it makes absolutely no difference in this life. The same is true, as well, for the reincarnation theory – coming back as a flower or bird or angel. Let's say you were somebody in a past life. Do you know who you were? No. Even if you did, you're not them right now; you're <u>you</u>. You experience yourself and live your life as you, as unique. So, it makes absolutely no difference if you were here before or not, either as you or as somebody or something else. And if you come back in the future, you will have no idea that you were around before. You'd just be the new you.

Another possibility for coming back physically would be to come back to <u>another</u> physical universe. But there isn't another universe. "Universe" by definition means everything that is. We don't even know the extent or boundaries of this one, if there are any. Of course, there could be much more matter outside of the "light cone" that Stephen Hawking talks about, but that is not within our capacity to know. It's unimaginable to us, so it really doesn't matter.

Do We Come Back Spiritually?

To explore whether we come back spiritually, let's explore what that life might be like. First, there would be no life as we know it, no physical being – no birth, growing or dying. There can't be any physicality unless there's birth, growth and death. The only way that planets and suns can be born is if others die, that plants can be born is if others die, that humans can be born is if others die. The stuff of the universe constantly gets recycled. The old batch has to die for the new batch to come along. Physicality implies birth and death. Our concepts of space, and therefore of time, exist because of physicality. No physicality means there would be no space and no time. It's hard to imagine what that "life" might look like.

We beg the question when we say: Isn't there a way that the non-physical part of us, our soul, could remain or endure? I can't imagine a "me," a soul, without my body. It seems to me there are no spirits around, only spirited beings. Once your body goes, you go. Yet, if this is so, why would people over the ages have invented such a concept as soul or spirit if there weren't any such thing? Precisely because we are afraid to think that death may be the end. We don't have the courage to be here now.

Likewise, with the question: Can't we stick around after death just as "being"? There are two problems. First, we now "be," are, as an "I"; but then we would just be part of one big, undifferentiated "being." It is our physicality that gives rise to our individuality. No physicality means no me. I'll be nobody because I'll have no body. Yet if I come back or continue to exist, I would want to be me as me, not just part of "us," not just part of "being," with no identity.

Of course, "being" may be ecstatic, not boring. Experiencing "being" is probably what theologians mean by the Beatific Vision. But then, what would this big, undifferentiated "being" know and do? Would we know just what's going on in the physical universe we left behind? But if we can't participate in the universe, that doesn't seem like much fun, does it? Maybe we'll just contemplate stuff like sunsets – or big-bang-sets. As you can see, this line of thinking doesn't lead anywhere.

The second and more important problem is, as I said in the last chapter, that all of my experience in this life shows that there is always something, a be-er, that "be's." You can't just have being, without somebody or something doing the being, somebody who "be's." It seems pretty impossible to have being without "be-ers" around. (Hey, there's a good image of heaven – "be-ers all around!") I can't envision what a soul or spirit might be, or how they would be, after death.

Hope

The concept of life is based on hope, so I also want to say a little about hope. Hope has gotten better press than it deserves. There are two ways of looking at hope, one bad and one good. Hope is bad when it prevents people from living in this world, when it prevents us from looking at what's so and taking control over our lives. It's bad when we say: This life isn't "it," the next life will be "it." On the other hand, hope is good when it provides value during this life. It provides the juice of anticipation – like when you buy lottery tickets or a stock. It gives you something to look forward to. It also carries with it the inspiration to do something to help you achieve what you hope for.

A further extension of hope is fantasy. I am a big fan of fantasy. Fantasy is fun because it stimulates the creative process which is fun in itself. But better that that, fantasies create possibilities where none existed before. They remove the parameters we set on our thinking about what's possible. The way it often works is that a fantasy can become a vision, which can become an outrageous goal, and then a realistic goal, and then an objective, and then a reality through action. Even if it doesn't lead anywhere, fantasy is good simply because it is fun and gives juice to life. However, like hope, it isn't good if it prevents us from taking responsibility for living in this world.

So, it is O.K. to fantasize about an afterlife. Here's mine: We all somehow get our bodies back at the best stage and condition in life (perhaps never even achieved while we were here)! Therefore, everybody is beautiful. And you can have sex with anybody and maintain the relationship as long as you both want. You could say: "Honey, we've been together for 200 years, and I'd kind of like to make it with Cleopatra." Of course, there's a 16 million year waiting list for Cleopatra, but what do you care? You've got the time. And when your honey leaves you, you never feel rejected because you know you've made it. You're in heaven, you're gorgeous and everybody sees your inherent beauty. Nobody could reject you. It's just that there is a line. There are plenty of other fish in the sea while you are waiting (if that is your thing – yes, you could even make it with Charley Tuna if you wanted to!)

So, here I am fantasizing about the afterlife! Given what I've just said, is that wrong? No, not if I don't let it affect how I live this life. Not if I don't do anything (or not do anything) based on the hope that my fantasies for life after death may come true.

In summary, it really doesn't matter in the long run whether there is an afterlife of not. Whether my death is my end, period, or whether I continue on in another state (perhaps Montana), that should not prevent me from living my life now to the fullest. Some people feel that if there were no reward and punishment, everybody would run amuck and do bad things in this life. However, I don't think so, as explained in the next chapter, **Morality and Love**.

Death as a Gift

The best I can say is that life is a gift, and death is a gift, because they are both part of what's so. In fact, we couldn't have life unless we have death. There is nothing in the universe that doesn't come into and then go out of existence. If flowers lived permanently, we would have no seeds. If we had only seeds, we would have no plants. If we had only plants we would have no fruits. On a human level, if nobody died on the planet, where would we put everybody? We actually would stop having children. So, for life we need death. Life and death are two sides to the coin of how the universe operates.

Ideally, we should look at death as we look at life. We need to somehow be able to say: "Oh boy, I am alive today. Oh boy, I die today." This may seem to be pushing it a bit, but look at it this way: we presume we have the right to exist, yet we don't. Our being here is a pure gift. If we live 90 years, it's a gift. If we live one day, it's a gift. If we die, it's a gift, because we had to live for at least one second in order to die. Everything is a gift, both life and death. Can we accept death as graciously as we accept life?

We are learning to congratulate people on getting a divorce, just as we congratulate them on getting married: "Congratulations on moving ahead with your lives!" When people make a decision that helps them to move forward in their lives, they should be congratulated. How about the same for death! But with death there is no future! In divorce you can say, "What a shame" or "it didn't work out" which means you are focusing on the past. With divorce we can focus on the future as well. But with death, that's all there is. There is no future. But maybe that's the point: The only reason we fear or dislike death is that we don't like the present and only want to look toward the future. The alternative is to love every minute of this game and play it as it goes. Another way of saying this is to say what Job said, "The Lord gives and the Lord takes away. Blessed be the name of the Lord."

I think that the acceptance of death is, in fact, the ticket to enjoying life. Knowing that we die points to the conclusion: Live life now, enjoy life now, savor each moment.

Get happy now! Lighten up and laugh. I think the essence of humor is: "Hey, what a joke. I thought I was in charge of the universe. I'm not in charge!" Of course, it's easy to say that when you are moving forward and things are going your way. When things go against your expectations, however, it is difficult to remember that this is the perfect time to lighten up, to laugh, and to say, "I am not in charge!" Isn't that what we should do at death as well? It is the ultimate admission of not being in charge. So, we should graciously accept the gift of death, which really means that we are reaffirming the gift of life; we affirm the whole package.

I think of Richard Thoen, a student I taught in Buffalo in the '60s saying at the end of his life, "I am not dying of AIDS; I'm living with AIDS." Spending your life waiting to die is the same as spending your life waiting to live. Perhaps there is no such thing as "dying." Better, dying takes place in only a split second. For all of the other hundreds of millions of seconds preceding it, we are living.

Summary

No one knows whether there is an afterlife. No one knows if we return to this life. But it seems unlikely. To have a physical afterlife would be contrary to all the ways physicality works now. It is our physicality that gives us individuality. If we came back as part of "being," we wouldn't be us, but just part of being. This is contrary to the way we understand things now, because we need "be-ers" to be. Since we can't know any of these things, it makes no difference. It shouldn't affect how we live this life. Life is freely given, and death is inherent in the concept of life. We should accept both graciously.

Chapter 12:

MORALITY AND LOVE

What is morality? What is love?

As I said earlier, the third reason people may believe in a god is that they think you need a god to be the source of morality – how people behave toward one another. It ties in with afterlife as well. God is going to reward the good guys and punish the evil ones after death. I believe, however, that morality has nothing to do with god or religion. That is, unless you look at it in reverse – people have done and still do incredibly cruel things to others in the name of god and religion!

I define morality as how we conduct our lives in relation to one another and toward everything else in the universe. It also applies to how I behave toward myself inasmuch as I should treat myself just as kindly as I treat other creatures. We use the word "love" to describe the natural way people interact with each other when the planet is functioning successfully. Love is linking ourselves harmoniously to the rest of the universe, living in harmony with the stars, the earth, and especially others. When we speak about love as the greatest commandment we have to realize that this is an oxymoron. If it's really love, then it can't be a commandment. If you're doing it because you're commanded to, it's not really love. A commandment is something somebody else tells you to do, that you don't really want to do. Love means you recognize or are willing to recognize the inherent quality in something or somebody else, and, recognizing the quality, you are attracted to or like and care about them. If you care about somebody because somebody else tells you to care about them, you don't really care about them.

Truthfully, though, aren't there some people that we really <u>don't</u> like or care about? Precisely. So we just need to admit that we don't love them. I hate the saying, "You have to love them but you don't have to like them." You can't love them without liking them. Why would you wish somebody well if you didn't like them? If it's because somebody else tells you to, then you're really not wishing them well; you're wishing <u>yourself</u> well. You're doing it for what you want to get out of it, which has nothing to do with them, or with love.

Let me back up a bit. There is some value in the "commandment" of love. That is, when we initially don't like someone, don't see their inherent value, it is useful to suspend that judgment. It is being willing to say that there is some inherent value in them, something lovable, and I am just not able to see it now. Since I am blinded, I am willing to give them the benefit of a doubt and treat them as if I did see their inherent value. After all, the universe has already voted on their basic goodness by putting them into existence. It has invested billions of years in creating their precise and unique genetic code and bringing it into fruition. When you see the value of someone or something else, you have a natural, outgoing attraction to that person or thing. They're not good because god says so; they're good because they're good, and you see it and like it. What if you don't see any good in someone else? You are wearing blinders. A guy has a big pimple on his nose, so all you see is a big pimple walking down the street. It's called "selective perception," which I talked about earlier. This even applies to Hitler. (I love bringing him in. It drives people crazy.) Hitler is just like us. He did the best he could.

Perhaps there are two levels of love then. The first is the level of reverence and respect for each thing in the universe, just because it is. This comes from the belief that if it is, it is good. The second level of love is actually seeing the value or goodness of another, and the natural response to that which is attraction to them and liking and caring about them.

The "Great Commandment," "Love one another," should really be called "The Great Reminder." In fact, all Ten Commandments from the bible are just "reminders." (You can check out my reinterpretations of them in the next chapter.) They, as all natural laws, are "ex post facto." That is, they come <u>after</u> seeing the way people operate in the most beneficial or harmonious manner, not <u>before,</u> as prescriptions of how people <u>should</u> operate. They are expressions of the natural order of things. Take the law of gravity, for example. Things don't fall because of the law of gravity. Rather, people invented the law of gravity as a way to describe the phenomenon: "things fall." (More precisely: things attract each other in inverse proportion to their mass.) Moral laws are simply a description of how people behave when things work in the best natural order – that is, work best for everybody, not just me. You don't kill or steal from or molest others because it's a commandment. The reason you don't do those things is that the other person or their relatives or friends or fellow citizens will kick your butt if you do. This is what we call "law." People sat down and described how things work best for everybody. Rather than everybody killing each other all the time we find that things work better if we get along with each other. We wouldn't do "bad" things even if there were no such thing as the ten commandments.

What about hardened criminals; don't they need commandments and laws to keep them in check? No. If laws and commandments kept them in check, they wouldn't have done bad things and they wouldn't be criminals! If you talk to a criminal – not in court or in an accusatory way – they wouldn't say: "Oh yeah, I think murdering and stealing are great. I love to do it." Rather they would say, "They're wrong and I wish I didn't do them. I wish I were constituted in such a way as to not be prone to do these things." It may sound as if I as saying that there are no such thing as "bad people." I am. There are just "people." What the universe has delivered is good – "God don't make no junk!" If people are here, they're good. If you don't see their goodness, you're just seeing pimples walking down the street – or behind bars. A better question is: "why do good people do bad things?" My theory is that people murder, or steal, or beat their children, or drink, or smoke, or call their kids "jerks" (like I do once in awhile) because of some kind of compulsion. But I am getting ahead of myself. Please see the chapters on **Good and Evil** and **Sin.**

The bottom line about morality is that it means I see the value in you. I respect and reverence you. I see our bond, our underlying unity. I see our planetary partnership and I'm happy to act appropriately toward you, to dance the appropriate dance with you, and likewise with everything in the cosmos. If we don't see this, our task is to open our eyes. The path of man is to see more and more the integral relationship of all things in the universe.

We really don't need a god to live "morally." We only need to open our eyes. We also need to give up victim mentality. Dragging god into the picture is what "victims" do, people who don't take responsibility for their lives and their actions. "I love you because god wants me to," or "I kill you because god wants me to," are equally irresponsible. We do what we do because we choose to do it, or we choose not to take responsibility to tackle the compulsion that has us do the things we don't want to. Stop playing god by trying to drag her into it!

Summary

Morality is how we behave toward everything in the universe, especially toward other people. The natural response to everything in the universe is called "love." The first level of love is to have reverence and respect for everything in the universe, just because it is. The second level of love is to actually see the attractiveness, value or goodness of another. Our natural response to that is to like, to care about, to reverence the other. We don't need to be commanded to love. In fact, if you love because you are commanded to, you are not loving. When people don't love others, it is because they are blinded to their natural goodness. When people do bad things, it is generally out of some compulsion. The Ten Commandments, the whole moral law, are not laws, not prescriptive ways of behaving. They are simply descriptions of the way people act when they are in harmony with the rest of the universe.

Chapter 13:

THE *NEW* TEN COMMANDMENTS

Should we still obey the Ten Commandments?

I think it's a good idea to obey the Ten Commandments, but with two conditions. First, they are out-dated and need to be reinterpreted. (What does "covet" really mean?) Secondly, as I said in the last chapter, we really aren't "commanded" to do them. They are more or less simply ways that people behave when things work best. As with many aspects of my old faith, I reinterpret the Ten Commandments in a way that makes sense to me now

On the next few pages I give my modern interpretations of the Ten Commandments. I had to do some digging into what I see as the essence of the old commandments to be able to apply them in a way that makes sense for me. You may feel that these are a stretch; if so, write your own! I am including the old Ten Commandments because I suspect that there is an inverse ratio between the level of righteousness in Christians and their ability to actually recite the Ten Commandments. (I was going to say "bad righteousness," but I wonder if there is any such thing as "good righteousness.") Besides, some Buddhists or Sufis might read this book and not know the original Ten Commandments. Finally, I use the Catholic version of them, which differs from Protestant versions.

THE OLD / NEW TEN COMMANDMENTS

1) Old: I am the Lord, thy God; thou shalt not have strange Gods before me.

   New:If you think you're indestructible, you're crazy. You had no say as to when or how you got here and no say about whether you're leaving or not. You didn't in vent this game; you and this whole game which you're part of is a gift to you. It doesn't make a differ ence to the universe or cosmos – or even an outie god if there is one – whether you remember this or ac knowledge it or not, but it may make a difference to you. So, acknowledge your creature-hood once in a while and rejoice in it.

2) Old: Thou shalt not take the name of the Lord, thy God, in vain.

   New: Don't say stupid things trying to deny command ment number one.

3) Old: Remember, thou keep holy the Lord's day.

   New: In fact, once in while sit down and think about what I said in number one. Try to appreciate the magnifi cence of the universe and the privilege it is to be playing in this game. Having a regular time to do this is not a bad idea.

4) Old: Honor thy father and thy mother.

   New: Your parents owe you nothing; you owe them everything. Don't act like a jerk toward them. Also, on the other hand, don't be afraid to face up to your true feelings and to share those feelings with them, whether you consider the feelings "negative" or "positive." As children, we childishly expect our parents to be everything, to be gods. We carry resentments about their humanness into later life, and we probably can't get over these resentments unless we communicate our feelings to our parents. It is then that we find out that, horror of horrors, we are exactly like our parents: we aren't omnipotent, we don't know everything and we are doing the best we can.

5) Old: Thou shalt not kill.

New: If you try to hurt or kill other people, they'll try to hurt or kill you. If not, somebody from their family will. If not, society will. Nobody wants to live in fear, looking over their shoulder all the time. So people band together to get rid of individuals who threaten others physically. When you're tempted to hurt somebody, think about it first. Besides, if you really had your eyes open you would love everybody, not want to kill them. And – do I have to say this? – an obvious corollary to not killing others is to not hurt them.

6) Old: Thou shalt not commit adultery.

New: This is an extension of number five – don't mess around sexually with someone who doesn't want to. It's the same as physically harming them. Also, make sure you don't have babies if you don't want them. Other than that, enjoy sex. It was the best present I could think of giving each and every one of you. This subject sells so many books, however, that I want to dedicate the whole next chapter to it. (Oops, I mean that I commanded Frank to write that chapter.)

7) Old: Thou shalt not steal.

New: The same applies to taking other people's stuff. If they're using it, you have to ask them first whether you can use it. If they say no, do something for them or give them something so that they'll be willing to let you use it. Remember, you don't own anything at all. None of you owns anything. All of this stuff is mine and I'm letting you use it while you are on the planet. You are only renting your home, your land, your body, all your goods. Spread my stuff around. If people hoard, set a good example for them by not doing it yourself. He who has the most toys when he dies loses.

8) Old: Thou shalt not bear false witness against thy neighbor.

New: Don't say what's not true. People will get upset with you, not work with you, not play with you, not have anything to do with you. They naturally don't want to hang around someone they can't trust, just as you don't. Shoot straight, even when it hurts. This is especially true of things you say about others.

Note from Frank:

God asked me to write two new commandments for numbers nine and ten. She is embarrassed that she didn't edit very well the first time around and just discovered that these last two are simply a repeat or reinforcement of numbers six and seven. Or, perhaps the guys who wrote the *Bible* liked to round off to ten, so they just stuck them in for a little padding. But for the sake of completeness, I will leave them in, explain them and then give two better ones.

9) Old: Thou shalt not covet thy neighbor's wife.

New: This is not really a commandment. It is a repeat of what I had to say in number six. If you have sex with someone who is married to someone else, even if you both thought it was a good idea, their (and your) spouse might not. Be careful; all three or four of you have a lot of talking to do before you get into this situ ation. I had a lot of people experiment with it in the '60s, and in the large majority of cases it just didn't seem to work.

Another way of looking at this commandment is that monogamy seems to work best in advanced societies. Don't dwell on sexual thoughts with people other than your own partner. It doesn't lead you in the right direction.

10) Old: Thou shalt not covet thy neighbor's goods.

New: I talked about this in number seven. When people say, "Don't even think about parking here," they are just emphasizing their point, "Don't park here!" Dwelling on what others have and you don't is only good if it gets you off your butt to go out and earn or create what you want. Otherwise, it leads to jealousy or even trying to take things from others against their will. Or, it can lead you to feeling like a victim. None of these is healthy.

Since these last two commandments are repeats, I am taking the liberty to invent two wholly new commandments for numbers nine and ten:

New #9) Don't make any commandments.

The above aren't commandments. They are natural ways of acting when you live in harmony with society, i.e., in a way that works for everybody. If someone decides to act in an unnatural way, your or my saying it's a commandment isn't going to make any difference. The thing you have to do is to love them, ask them why they're doing it, and try to get down to the underlying feeling and need which is causing their aberrant behavior.

New #10) Lighten up!

This is my most serious commandment! The more you

laugh, the more you are acknowledging your "creature-hood," and the more healthily you can move forward.

After what I said earlier, it might have been better to call these "The Ten Suggestions" or "Ten Reminders of the Right Way to Act" or "Ten Things That Go On When The World Is Functioning In A Way That Works For Everybody." But the writers of the bible got a head start on me, so I have stuck with "Commandments" and tried to reinterpret them in a way that makes sense to me.

Summary

The Ten Commandments are ancient ways of saying what everybody knows is the natural, practical, expedient way to behave toward the earth and one another. The new ones are interpretations that are more in line with how we (specifically, I) think today.

Chapter 14:

THE SIX SEX COMMANDMENTS

Is sex good or bad?

That depends on whom you are having it with! Seriously, sex is not only good but absolutely necessary and absolutely wonderful. Where would we all be without it? Yet, if sex is good, why do we have so many hang-ups (I'm not talking about 900 numbers here) about it?

One problem is that some people think that pleasure is bad. That is, seeking pleasure for its own sake is bad. They think that if you have sex just for pleasure and not procreation (making babies), that's bad. Where could such a thought come from? My theory is that, for Christians, this perversion goes back to the "Virgin" Mary. Early Christian scripture writers were very big on trying to make Jesus into god. So, they made Mary into a virgin, because this would "prove" Jesus was conceived by god. Later Christians thought: "Oh, virginity must be good. So, sex must be bad – or at least to be just tolerated for the sake of procreation." People's own sexual hang-ups got into the act, like Paul saying, "It's better to marry than to burn in hell," and other such inanities. (I am not saying, by the way, that it is better to burn in hell than to marry!) Just a guess as to where the silly "sex is bad" notion came from.

My opinion is that sexual pleasure for its own sake is not only O.K.; it's actually rather nice! Sex has gotten such a bad name in most religions, that I have invented a little scenario of how it got invented: When god created people he said, "What's the best gift I can give them that would be extremely enjoyable, free, available to everyone every day, and requiring no other resources (except hands, etc.)? That's why he invented orgasm. Then, being interested in efficiency, he said, "How could I also use it to help two people to form a loving relationship?" Then he said, "Hot damn! How could I also use this to create offspring as well?" This is how he invented sex.

Sexual morality, as with all other morality, comes from the principle of not hurting others. As I said earlier, the principle of not hurting anyone is a description of how things work when they work best for everybody. That is why I have made up the six sex commandments, oops, rules, oops, descriptions of how people act when they act in a way that works best for everybody. They all have to do with not hurting others, and not hurting yourself. The brilliant thing about them is that they are in a hierarchical order. That means if you don't observe #6, at least make sure you observe the other 5. If you don't pay attention to #s 5 and 6, at least follow the other 4, and so on. Obviously, #1 is the most important. I will give you all six first, then discuss them. Let's call them "commandments" for convenience.

THE SIX SEX COMMANDMENTS

1. Don't have babies unless you want them and can take care of them.

2. Don't hurt others: Don't give others AIDS, venereal disease or other sexually transmitted diseases; don't coerce anyone into having sex, or hurt another for sex.

3. Don't get these diseases yourself or allow yourself to be forced into having sex (unless it is to

prevent bodily harm to yourself), or to be hurt by another.

4. Don't have sex if it violates any of your principles, or if you don't feel good about it.

5. Don't unnecessarily upset your spouse, parents, or others by having sex.

6. Don't have sex if you really don't like the person.

Starting with commandment or principle #1, the primary source of all sexual taboos is to prevent the birth of children people don't want or can't take care of. If sex didn't have anything to do with babies, we'd have no problem with it – other than the other five principles. Use of condoms handles this and also the part of principle #2 that says not to get AIDS or other sexually transmitted diseases as well.

Principles #2 and #3 simply say, "Don't hurt others or your-self." Principle #2 comes before #3 because it's more impor-tant to not mess up other people's lives than to not mess up your own. That's what "morality" is all about, how we re-late to others. If you were a hermit living in a cave some-where, "morality" would have no meaning. Of course, you have to be "moral" toward yourself, to respect yourself. But we wouldn't call it morality. We wouldn't say, "Let's see; I want to hit myself in the head with a rock, but I have this rule etched on the cave wall that says not to." You just wouldn't do dumb things to yourself on purpose. I include principle #3 because of how I defined morality – doing what works best for everybody. You are somebody, part of the "ev-erybody," so you count too. Not hurting others or yourself in the area of sex or anything else is just common sense.

If #s 1, 2 and 3 are common sense principles, why do so many not heed them? Why do we act stupidly? Some an-swers are: we are too horny to control ourselves; too lazy to use carry and use birth control protection; too needy or wanting to be liked; too young and inexperienced, and so on. We sacrifice long term good for short term good, which is what we do when we act immorally in any area. Some, especially adolescent girls, don't have a very good self-image. They want to be loved, liked, accepted by others. They are needy for love. So many young teenagers seem to have children out of wedlock today, and I think it is because they don't have very much sense of self-worth: "If I have a baby, then I will be important – at least to the baby." They don't realize they will be radically altering their life by having a child. It takes a huge amount of energy and courage to raise a child. So, they are willing to have sex to gain what seems to affirm them, but then pay a huge price in either abortion, adoption or 18 years of responsibility for raising a child. (That is, if their daughter doesn't go out and have a child without being married, so that now they get to raise <u>two</u> children – their own and their grandchild!)

Principle #4 is, don't have sex if it violates any of your principles or if you don't feel comfortable about it. If you have a principle of "no sex before marriage," then follow it. If you have a principle of having fun in a mutually agreed on and safe way, do that. Don't do anything you are not comfortable with. On the other had, don't be afraid to take risks either. I dare say that when most people have sex for the first time, they don't feel entirely comfortable. You'll just have to decide on your own comfort/risk level.

Principle #5 is about not upsetting others. I am talking about third parties (not menage a trois), people involved other than the one you're having sex with. If you are considering having sex with someone other than your spouse, obviously that doesn't work well for society. Spouses get angry and take revenge or leave you or don't trust you any more, and so on. Monogamy just seems to work better. Likewise, if you are a teenager living with your parents, you should consider their feelings. You have to make the final judgment about what you do, but their feelings and desires are part of what you should consider.

Principle #6 is sort of an extension of principle #2. If you don't have some attraction to the person, then you are just using them, and they will know it. So, you need to take their feelings into consideration as well. If two people are horny, know they have no commitment to each other and consider #'s 1 to 5, then go for it!

What about masturbation? As you can see, it has nothing to do with these 6 principles, because they all have to do with sex in relation to others. Masturbation is a solitary act and harms no one. As a matter of fact, is probably very helpful to most people! As I said earlier, pleasure for its own sake is not a bad idea. It is actually a good idea!

What about homosexuality? Researchers are coming to discover that homosexuality, as well as ADD, depression, etc., are genetically transmitted. In other words, many – perhaps all – gay people can't help being gay. One of my gay friends told me, "Do you think I would choose this lifestyle if I had a choice about it?" In fact, I wish more men were gay. That is, "gay" in the old sense of the word – they acted gaily, they weren't afraid to be expressive, lively, spontaneous, gleeful. Generally, men are afraid to express these traits, their feminine side. Gays offer a real value to the rest of us men. In short, regardless of sexual orientation, I wish men were more open and expressive, including myself. I also wish more lesbians were.

What about prostitution? If it doesn't violate any of the 6 principles, then it is okay. The question comes up, isn't it always demeaning, hurtful to the prostitute to sell sexual favors? I don't know the answer to that. Doctors, dentists, masseurs, etc. use their bodies to touch our bodies, and it has positive results. In one sense, you could say that prostitutes are coerced into doing it because of financial necessity. Then again, think of how many workers are "coerced" into doing things they don't want to do because they have to make a living. Imagine if you had to be a telemarketer! I presume there are some prostitutes who like what they do, but I suspect most don't and don't do it for very long. The positive side of prostitution is that it serves people who want to have sex but can't get it, or enough of it, through normal channels. Perhaps there is less rape and other sexual coercion as a result, as in the Scandinavian cultures. Perhaps there are just a lot of happier people as a result! Certainly, it should not be criminalized, since it is a victimless "crime." On the other hand, pimping clearly seems criminal, since it is a form of coercion.

Finally, there is one burning question that many Christians have about sex: Is it all right to have intercourse before receiving communion? The answer is yes, as long as you don't block the aisles.

Summary

Most of the taboos around sex arise from the need for society to not have unwanted babies. All of the morality around it stems from this and from the principle of not hurting others or yourself. The six "commandments" outline the conclusions from these principles in a hierarchical order.

Chapter 15:

HOW TO RESOLVE THE ABORTION QUESTION

Is abortion good or bad?

This is one of the most passionate topics of our day. There are two considerations. First, is abortion the same as "hurting someone?" Is it the same as destroying an unborn person? The second, broader consideration abortion brings up is whether or to what degree one segment of society can impose its moral judgment on another. To answer the first question, let's look at it in the context of other beliefs surrounding sex, birth, life and death. This will enable us to get a perspective.

Concerning sex, birth and death I want to distinguish nine levels of action about which people make moral judgments. Each level can be said to be "good" or "bad." These levels are in a hierarchy. That means you can draw the line under any number in the hierarchy and say: Everything above this line is bad; everything below it is okay. As with any other belief, you can find reasons to justify drawing the line at any level. As you read these levels, ask yourself where you would draw the line: "Is this bad, evil, or not?" Here they are:

1. Putting an adult to death.

2. Putting a new-born to death.

115

3. Putting a baby to death just before birth.

4. Putting a baby (fetus) to death who could survive outside the womb.

5. Putting a baby (fetus) to death who could survive outside the womb only with extraordinary medical support.

6. Destroying a fetus which would have no viability outside the womb at all.

7. Destroying a fertilized human egg.

8. Preventing a sperm from reaching an egg (i.e., birth control)

9. <u>Wanting</u> to prevent a sperm from reaching an egg; that is, wanting to have sex for pleasure only and not procreation, whether or not you actually have it.

People on the planet draw lines below or above every single level in this hierarchy, saying that what is above the line is wrong and what is below is okay. Where do <u>you</u> draw the line? Some even draw the line above #1. "Who?" you might ask. The answer is people who believe in capital punishment. But that's different, right? As I said, you can always find a reason to justify your point of view!

Similarly, some people draw the line below #2. For example, I understand that in India, some people still put newborn female infants to death. They do not feel that this is wrong because they value male infants more highly. But that is extreme, right? Well, things are extreme or not extreme depending on where you draw the line. "Extremeness" is relative. If we go, for example to the other "extreme," #9, even <u>thinking</u> about having sex for pleasure is wrong. ("Don't even <u>think</u> about parking [it] here.") When I was raised as a Catholic I was taught that if you wanted to do something "bad" and didn't actually do it, you still committed a sin. "Lusting in your heart" was as bad as doing it for real. There were three conditions for a mortal sin: a serious matter, sufficient reflection and full consent. If you had all three, you were guilty – even if you didn't actually <u>do</u> the thing. So, if you just thought about having sex with someone other than with your spouse and not for the purpose of procreation, you had a serious matter and sufficient reflection. Then, if you thought: "Yes, by golly, I would like to do such a thing if I had the chance," (full consent) then you're a bad boy. If you died after thinking such a thing, you would go straight to hell (and not pass "Go"). I am being a little sarcastic here, but there are Catholics who still believe this today – the Pope for one. They would draw the line under #9, meaning that everything on the whole list is bad, #s 1 through 9. Others would draw the line below #8 – birth control is wrong, and so on.

The point I am making here, and in this whole book for that matter, is that belief is relative. There is no absolute answer for where to draw the line. One can create a rationale for drawing it at any level, but the ultimate reason anyone can give for drawing the line where they do is this: "Because I say so." It is, as with any other belief, a matter of choice. The difference between people, though, is that some are tolerant and some are intolerant. Intolerance is bred by fear. Tolerant people say, "let's compare our reasons for drawing the line where we do and see if we can come up with some kind of practical way of making decisions about this." Intolerant people say, "here is where I draw the line, it is the right and only place, and there is no discussion about it." They use the rationale that god or the pope or their mom said that this is where the line must be drawn. They find it hard to see that the fundamental reason they are making this choice is simply because they say so.

Where do I personally draw the line between right and wrong? Theoretically, between 5 and 6. That is, putting a baby (fetus) to death who could survive outside the womb is wrong, and everything below that line is not. Practically speaking, however, if it were <u>my</u> child/fetus we were talking about, I have no idea what decision I would make. I

117

have, however, given up numbers 6 to 9 forever (well, I would be open to hearing any new points of view on these issues that I haven't heard before). You notice how my language shifted, going from #5 to #7? I went from "baby" to "fetus" and from "kill" to "destroy." Our choice of words tips off where we stand. The phrase "kill a baby" already has moral judgment built into it.

Morally speaking, then, how does one decide where to draw the line? One decides, period. More importantly, how do people who draw the line at different levels come to agree/compromise with each other when community action needs to be taken? The sticking points for most people in our society are below number 3 and above number 8. There are good, sincere, loving, wise, people who draw their line at all different points in this hierarchy.

Why are some people so intolerant of others who draw the line in a different place? Fear is my answer. They are afraid to admit that some of their views are relative and not absolute. It fits in with the mentality of people who kill killers. (Play with that one for a while!) Why are pro-life people are so adamant about, "Where I draw the line is the only place anyone may draw the line"? I have a theory, which comes from my experience as a Catholic. I used to believe that if the pope said something was right or wrong, then it was. The pope has the last say on matters of faith or morals. If you questioned it, you were putting yourself above the official teaching of the church. So, to make a decision to draw a line someplace different than the official teaching of the church, is very traumatic. It means that I, rather than the church, am now becoming the arbiter of my morality. If you question this piece of the church's teaching, then you question the basis for all its teaching. It shakes the very foundations of your belief system, of your being. This is very traumatic. Catholics and others don't question one piece, because they think that the whole foundation will fall if they make their own judgment about it.

However, I think there are three kinds of denial going on in this situation:

- Catholics don't face the fact that there isn't one seamless "Catholic" belief system but many Catholics whose beliefs are not 100% consistent with those of others.

- Worse yet, they don't face up to their own personal inconsistency between what they say they believe and how they act. They practice birth control, or seek revenge rather than turn the other cheek, or get divorced. Then they avoid coming to a resolution about the inconsistencies. I have the perverse thought of making up bumper stickers that say: "Pro-Lifer for Capital Punishment."

- They don't admit, as I said earlier, that the bottom line for why they hold any belief is because they choose to. They pretend they believe because god says so, but it is really because <u>they</u> say so.

However, even if all Catholics believed and practiced the same things, they also teach freedom of conscience This means you are free to draw the line anywhere your conscience tells you. This creates an inherent inconsistency: do what we tell you, but do what your conscience tells you. In practice, the church leadership really gets upset if you don't draw the line where <u>they</u> want you to (again, depending on <u>which</u> leader you are talking to). They are very much more vocal in their teachings about sex than their teachings about conscience. I guess this is so because the leadership is so defensive about sex. They are celibate men making rules about something they don't have (or, according to their rules, <u>shouldn't</u> have) any experience with, i.e., sex. If they started changing their views about sex, they would call into question the whole idea of celibacy. The horrible thought comes up, "Maybe celibacy is not an absolute rule. Maybe I gave up my sexuality for nothing!" This is not an easy thought to face. Better to defend it to the death than say, "Oh, we made a mistake," or, "that idea had some value in its time but it's time to change the rule now." I wonder how much of a decline will take place in Catholicism before necessity makes them say, "Maybe women and married priests are not such a bad idea."

I try to avoid labels about people, especially the labels "pro-life" and "pro-choice." In my experience, labels serve to divide people more than any good they do. They imply, "I am this, and you're not," with the "you're not" part being the most important. Being pro-life doesn't mean that you are against choice or individual conscience. Being pro-choice doesn't mean you don't reverence life. Values are underneath both of these beliefs, and the job with any belief is to uncover the value. As a civil society we need to have debate, respect others, and then make laws (or not) about drawing the line above #1, or # 2, or at whatever level we decide. As individuals, we need to pursue integrity, by getting clearer about our core values and aligning our beliefs, speech and actions with those values.

Summary

Abortion is obviously not desirable. Its "rightness" or "wrongness" is a matter of individuals coming to their own conclusions and the human community coming to consensus. Humans disagree as to where to draw the line in the nine-step hierarchy of actions. To some, me, the rational approach would be to say that before a fetus has viability outside of the womb it is a fetus, not a person. After it has viability it is a baby. Most agree that it is wrong to kill babies. We need to recognize the relativity of our beliefs, the values behind them, and to come to civil conclusions through civil discourse.

Section 4:

ABOUT HOW TO LIVE LIFE

Chapter 16:

GROWING UP

What does it mean to grow up? Why am I asking this question here?

Earlier I discussed how we perceive selectively, how we interpret what we perceive and how we inherit other people's interpretations/beliefs/stories as well. It is the clinging to these beliefs and not being willing to re-examine them that gets us in trouble, both personally and collectively. Part of my definition for "growing up" is to do just the opposite. We are "grown up" when we are able to step back and reevaluate beliefs and behaviors that we have inherited or chosen, and then to freely choose. I am speaking about growing up here, because it may give you a path to re-examine your beliefs. Let's explore this.

Why the unexamined life is not worth living

How can people interpret things so differently in life? Why we are even willing to die or kill for our beliefs? Part of the answer is that many of our beliefs come from our past. We don't formulate our stories, interpretations and conclusions about life in adulthood with our minds as blank slates. We come to each situation in life carrying attitudes with us. Every fundamental attitude we have was formulated in childhood, either by us or by others. We made life decisions based on interpretations we made as 4 or 7 or 10 year olds, and we bought into others' – primarily our parents' – interpretations of life. We grow up thinking that these are facts, data, rather than a story made up about the data. Most of these serve us well, but others may get us in trouble. I love the story of the husband who asked his wife why she always cut an inch off of the ham before she baked it. She said her mother always did it. So she called her mother and asked her why she did it. Her mother said, "I don't do that." The daughter: "Yes you do. When we were kids, you always did it." Her mother says, "Oh, that was before I bought a bigger pan!"

Let me give you a real life example. My mother, who was an Italian immigrant, always used to cut off a little bit of the end of a cucumber and then rub it on the rest of the cucumber. Foam would gather around the outside of the cucumber, and she said that this took away the bitterness. About 20 years after she passed away I remember having a discussion with my five sisters on whether any of them still rubbed tops of cucumbers! Most of them laughed, but one sister said that she had tested the theory and had determined that the practice indeed did take the bitterness out of cucumbers, so she continued doing it.

This is a somewhat trivial example, but it is a good illustration. For many years it was a fact in my family that rubbing the end of a cucumber took away the bitterness. It took a while for me to realize that this was just a story. Perhaps the story is true, but I have no scientific evidence for it and don't intend to pursue testing that belief. There were other stories in my childhood that were not so innocent but actually detrimental, and it took me many years to recognize the lack of utility for these stories and to drop them. For instance, that sex was bad, or at least just to be tolerated for the sake of creating children. I must say, happily, that I have given up that story because it no longer serves me.

Often in life, the belief or story comes first, and then we look for evidence to corroborate it. We look to justify what we already "know" or do. Two people can take the same external data and draw different conclusions. For example, if you believe in UFOs and you see a light in the sky at night, you might be inclined to label it a UFO. However, if you are sure there are no such things as UFOs and you see the same light, you'll interpret it as an airplane, a reflection, or something else in your experience. On a deeper level, if you are a Democrat you almost automatically discount what a Republican says, and vice-versa. On a most serious level, if you were abused as a child, you are very likely to grow up as a child abuser. Why? This is your experience of child rearing; this is all that you know about how parents raise children and you live according to what you know.

One of the biggest discoveries I made, when I was about 20, was that people don't generally think about a rational course of action and then act on it. Quite the contrary, we act and then make up a rational explanation for what we do. In other words, doing precedes thinking. Unless we pull back and re-evaluate the attitudes which the doing comes out of, doing precedes thinking for the rest of our lives! I realized this when I was thinking about the concept of loving others, and I realized that I couldn't <u>not</u> love others! Of course, my concept of loving others at that time meant to be nice or friendly toward them, to wish them well, and to try to do good for them if possible. I was amazed to realize that I really didn't have much choice about this, that my entire natural inclination was to be nice toward people, to please them. I couldn't imagine myself being otherwise or acting otherwise. It wasn't because I was following the Christian precept of "love one another," as if I were free to choose – "let's see, be nice or be mean? I think I'll be nice today." I was cast into that mold. I am, by the way, happy that my bent was toward niceness rather than meanness, but niceness isn't all that it is cracked up to be. I also realized that when another didn't reciprocate my rule of being nice, especially when I was nice to them, I became angry with the other person! My niceness had an unwritten price tag – the demand that you reciprocate!

So being rational is not very far from rationalizing. We act first and think secondly because that is the natural way things happen. We didn't drop on to the planet as fully seeing, fully thinking adults. We got dropped here as non-thinking beings. As one-year-olds we didn't discuss the pros and cons of having more than two children in a family, or nuclear disarmament. In fact, we developed innumerable patterns of action in childhood without any thought about the rationality or rightness about them. Of course, that didn't stop us from rationalizing any behavior, as my kids are experts at doing right now: there is a reason that I broke that chair, hit my brother, keep all the tools in my room, etc. I love the story where my wife discovered my son Ian's homework was due the previous day. She said, "This was due yesterday." He responded, "It's not the yesterday you think it is."

The capacity to know that we know only dawns slowly on us, so we are into semi-adulthood when we finally recognize this. By that time we have accumulated an immense amount of stories or beliefs that we have presumed were the only way to interpret life all these years. And that is the problem: perhaps what we have held is so, just isn't so. Perhaps this world is not flat, and there aren't monsters over the edge when we fall into the abyss.

It is only after growing up – in fact, this is precisely my definition for "growing up" – that we are able to step back and reevaluate beliefs and behaviors. Many of our behaviors and the rationale for them come from our parents, perhaps even our genes. We become adults when we are able to verbalize our values and goals and to recognize and deal with behaviors that are inconsistent with them. Maybe a better way of saying this is that we become adults when we admit that rationalization is the human condition, that we are creatures of habit long before the use of reason, and that we say what we do is right rather than ask what is right and then do it. Once we realize this, then we see that adulthood is a non-ending path of being willing to step back and reevaluate. It is only then we are free to choose rather than bound to choose.

When I say that "growing up" is the process of challenging beliefs, I am not talking about challenging others' beliefs, which most of us are excellent at doing, but challenging our own. There is a place for lovingly challenging others' beliefs as well, but it is difficult and tricky. I love the story of how Socrates got into so much trouble for questioning everybody. As I remember it, he went to the Oracle at Delphi and asked, "Who is the wisest man in the world, that I may go and learn from him?" The Oracle responded, "You are, Socrates." Now, Socrates knew he definitely was not very wise, but he also knew that the Oracle did not lie. So he set out to find someone wiser than himself. He questioned the politicians, the philosophers, the craftsmen, the reputedly wise, and he found that when he dug two or three levels deep with his questions, no one really knew very much about what they were talking about – other than the artisans knowing about their crafts. Unfortunately, people don't like to be shown that they don't know what they are talking about, so he made a lot of enemies. However, he came to realize that the Oracle was right, because, as he says, "I must be the wisest because, whereas I know that I don't know anything, others don't even know that they don't know anything." This is why he said, "The unexamined life is not worth living."

Challenging beliefs is difficult. It goes contrary to how we operate. Yet it is the source of each living his own life, not another's. Some people may be nervous when I talk about challenging beliefs, because they fear something will be taken away from them. But challenging beliefs is really a win-win situation. When you challenge something, there are two possibilities: If you discover it is no longer useful and give it up, it's because you have found, or are seeking, a more all-encompassing belief. If you keep the challenged belief, you become further strengthened in it. And that belief now becomes a matter of true choice, not one of unquestioned choice.

I remember studying theology where I believed certain doctrine, and I tried to relate new data that I experienced to it. For example, "How do we explain free will in the light of god's omnipotence?" In this example, we need to ask: what do you mean by "free will?" What do you mean by "omnipotence?" What do you mean by "God?" (Why do you capitalize "God?") and so on. This is where the most important learning takes place. It comes about when we challenge assumptions. The more fundamental the assumptions, the more powerful the learning. This is what I have done for myself in this book. It represents the learning that I have come up with in challenging all of the key assumptions concerning Catholicism, Christianity, religion and belief in general. As I said earlier, I encourage you to do the same.

Socrates didn't mean that we should go around re-examining all of our beliefs all the time. When should one re-examine their beliefs? The time to examine beliefs is when they create conflicts, when they don't seem to be working in our favor any more. Perhaps the best clue that it is time to re-evaluate is when the belief is turning us against other people. The outcome of re-examining our beliefs might be that we give them up or that we reaffirm and strengthen them. People are often afraid to re-evaluate their beliefs, but you can only be strengthened by the process. It certainly costs something to give up the belief, but the ultimate payoff is worth it. After I left the monks, I was in a "belief-less," empty state for about three or four years. With the help of therapy I finally got out of the state, and I have to say that I am much happier being on this side of my childhood beliefs rather than still stuck in them. This is not to say that I have given up all those beliefs. In fact I have reaffirmed some of them. For example, I am a very strong believer in, "do unto others as you would have them to unto you." But now it is much more of a choice on my part now rather than a compulsion.

Summary

"Growing up," in part, means to be willing to challenge the beliefs we grew up with, so that we can freely determine our own lives. When we examine them we can then re-affirm, revise, expand or drop them. It is then that we have freer and freer choice.

Chapter 17:

SPIRITUALITY

What is spirituality?

As I said in the **God** chapters, it seems that you can't separate "spiritual" from "physical." Yet, the word "spiritual" does have meaning. I often hear people say, "I am not religious, but I am spiritual." People don't subscribe to a specific religion or church, but they do consider themselves spiritual. But what does "spiritual" mean? As with so many other concepts in this book and in life, we think we know what something means, but only when we dig down into what we mean by it do we come to really discover it.

I have been struggling with the question of whether I am spiritual or not. On the one hand I have been described as a man of faith. My wife says I am one of the most Christian non-believers she knows. On the other hand, a fundamentalist who reads this book may say I am a man totally lacking in faith or spirituality. So, what is it that I want to create this word to mean to me? I phrase it that way because we have a predisposition towards words as positive, negative or neutral. I think of "spiritual" as positive – it is good to be spiritual. So I define it in a way that is positive for me. If one thought of the word as negative, then they would define it in a way that describes what they don't want to be, e.g., if you were a Democrat describing a Republican.

A brief digression on overcoming prejudice. Here's how

129

to do it: if you feel a word is negative, pretend it is a positive and then create a definition that makes sense in a positive way for you. Why would you want to do this? To link yourself with those who don't think the way you do, who have different beliefs. Then you get to see the value behind their beliefs. This doesn't negate the value of your beliefs; it takes you out of narrow "either-or" thinking into "both-and" thinking. For example, if you hate "liberals" you can pretend that "liberal" is a good word, a positive, and then redefine it in a way that is acceptable to you. That is what gets you in touch with the underlying values of "those liberals." An inclusive question that will allow you to encompass your beliefs as well as others' is; in what way is this a positive word for me, and in what way is it a negative word?

Getting back to creating a positive meaning for the word "spiritual," I go back to the original meaning of the word "spiritus," meaning "breath." If you extend the idea, you can take it back a step to "vitality," and take that back to "the energy force in the universe." A more detailed way of saying it is the "forward thrust or intelligent force in the evolutionary unfolding and development of the universe." I find it easier to think of "spiritual" as the force/energy/vitality that is the nature of everything we witness in the universe. I can then define spirituality as the unifying thread that pervades everything in the universe, which is the forward thrust or push to further development and fulfillment of being.

Given this definition, everything that participates in the universe is spiritual, each thing in its own fashion. When applying spirituality to humans, part of that forward thrust is consciousness: knowing and knowing that we know. From this point of view, everybody can then be considered spiritual as well. Given the range of human beings, our spirituality, or consciousness, varies. Some of us are "less evolved" than others. With that consciousness comes linking ourselves to the rest of the universe, living in harmony with the stars, the earth, others. This is what love means.

What would be some characteristics of an evolved "spiritual" person? I have come up with seven so far – and it has been fun doing so, because it really has gotten me to create a picture of who I want to be. Spiritual persons:

1. Are conscious of our inter-relatedness with everything in the universe.

2. Are conscious of our grandeur and, at the same time, of our smallness. That is, conscious of the immense privilege it is to participate in the universe, wherein we get to create our own role in its coming to be more fully. And also conscious of what a finite speck we are in its vastness.

3. Participate as fully as possible in the goods of the universe, yet understand the maelstrom that attachment and accumulation can sweep us into. This understanding demonstrates itself in sharing of these gifts with others. We allow the gifts of the universe to flow to us and through us.

4. Genuinely like, care for, and are interested in others.

5. Have a sense of humor. Death helps out with this: Now you see me, now you don't.

6. Have lifelong curiosity, inquisitiveness, desire to learn and grow.

7. Are able to go placidly into the crowd, or into themselves.

As you can see, I have made up a list of the qualities that I like, all of which have to do with linking us up with the bigger picture, the universe. Yet the question comes up, doesn't spiritual mean something like "your soul," the you that exists apart from your body? I don't think so. That's the meaning most people would have for the word, but I have a hard time with that. It's hard to think of "soul" without a body to go with it. If you go back to the origin of the word spirit, it's hard to think of "breath" without a breather. "Soul" is not a "thing," not something that has a separate and distinct existence. It does have a "reality." That is, when we use the word it points to something in our experience. I think that the reality it points to is our hope for an afterlife. Most people find it unpalatable to think that when our body goes we go. (You mean this life was <u>not</u> a dress rehearsal?) So, if there is a "thing" that will persist, a soul or spirit, we feel better because our body pretty clearly disintegrates. However, as I discussed in the chapter on **Afterlife**, an afterlife is something we can't know about, and it is a dubious concept to me.

Summary

Each of us needs to define "spiritual" for ourselves. As I see it at this point in my life - and imposing a positive meaning on the word - "spirituality" means to recognize our inter-relatedness with the universe and the part we play in the forward thrust of the universe. I have listed some of my values in life above, and apply the name "spiritual" to them.

Chapter 18:

HOLINESS

What is holiness?

Most people link the concept of holiness to their concept of god – holiness is being like god, or being in a way that a god would want us to be. The old saying: "God made man in his image and likeness, and man returns the compliment." I used to think this was so clever until I surmised that god has no reality except in human invention. But this counts for a lot. The concept of holiness is important because it becomes a description of the ideal we strive for, our description of the highest values in life. A holy person is the highest evolution of a spiritual person. The real question is: What should we, I, strive for in life? Or, since I advocate getting rid of the word "should," what are the highest values that I want to pursue in life? This is a more vital question, and it helps shed old connotations of holiness which are no longer useful.

Some of the old connotations I don't like about "holiness" are:

1. Being passive, in the guise of patience or humility.
2. Being victimized by letting other people or things control you.
3. Counting on life having its meaning and fulfillment in the next world, not this one.
4. Thinking there is some pre-ordained path in life for each individual.
5. Being "not of this world," that is, not taking part in

the world, but being "above" it.
6. Being naive.

In re-inventing holiness to my liking, I would say that a holy person has these characteristics:

1. Courage – the courage of a Ghandi who does what's right in the face personal danger.
2. Vision – the vision of a Ghandi to free a people – two peoples in fact – and the dogged pursuit of that vision.
3. Service – the being of service to others, or as Shaw says, "to be used for a purpose recognized by your self as a might one."
4. Joy – a deep sense of satisfaction about yourself, about everybody, about life.
5. Peace – doing all of the above naturally, without stress or sacrifice or burden.

In one sense, no one is holy because no one exhibits all of these qualities. In fact, even Ghandi and Mother Theresa didn't all the time. They had their bad moments too. So I like this as a new definition of holiness: if you are <u>striving</u> for these qualities, approaching these qualities, then you can be called holy. In that case, anybody who espouses these qualities and is doing the best they can is holy. So, welcome to the brotherhood of the canonized!

Summary

The word "holiness" describes the highest qualities or attributes humans strive for. I describe the most important ones to me above. Since this is such a short chapter, I am not going to repeat them.

Chapter 19:

GOOD AND EVIL

What is good and what is evil?

That depends. First let's make a distinction. We use these words in three different areas:

1. How people behave toward one another
2. How the universe operates
3. How an individual may be good or evil

I have already talked about the first category, good and evil in terms of how humans behave toward each other, in the chapter on **Morality and Love**. In this chapter I will discuss the second, good and evil in how the universe operates. In the next chapter, I will talk about the concept of a person being good or evil.

Looking at the whole universe, what is good and what is evil? I think most people would agree that everything is good. Nothing is evil. The universe is good just because it is; it exists. It is better to be than not to be. Of course, this is just a belief, a value judgment, on my part. One could just as easily say everything is evil; life is bad. But only people who are not happy with their own life would say that. Most people feel it is better to be than not to be.

What we sometimes call evil in the universe is the absence of good, and sometimes it's the universe functioning in a way contrary to our desires, plans or expectations. To illustrate the first type of "evil" let's take the example of light and darkness. Only one of those really exists (take a guess!). Darkness is the absence of light. Light exists, and darkness is what we call it when light isn't present. There really is no "is-ness" to darkness. Only light "is." Darkness can't be evil because it doesn't even exist. It's just a word we use to describe where light isn't. (There is a niggling thought in the back of my head that those who understand quantum physics might have different things to say about this.) Another type of absence of good in the universe is cold – the absence of heat. Cold is what we call a situation when heat, or enough heat, is absent. But these are relative terms. They're relative to human needs and perceptions. Without humans, the universe wouldn't know it's 200 degrees below zero in a particular location. A side thought: I wonder if absolute zero can ever be reached? Is there any such thing as absolute? Could the same question apply to light and darkness as well. Is there any such thing as absolute darkness, or absolute light?

Bringing things back down to earth, so to speak, can't we say earthquakes, for instance, are evil? But this looks at earthquakes from a limited perspective. From a global perspective, earthquakes are good: The universe is good. The earth is good. Plate tectonics is good. The rubbing of the plates up against each other is good. The shaking of my house is good. Whoops, did I go too far? No; I and my house just happened to be in the way of the universe evolving as it should. It's just that this isn't what I had planned. From our limited point of view, we call things natural "disasters" – earthquakes, floods, tornadoes, etc. – but they aren't evil. They are just part of the way the universe functions. We just have to stop being myopic. We should not look at these things as "natural disasters." They are natural, but not disasters.

Along with this point, we call beautiful sunrises or sunsets good. I think it is good to live here in Santa Barbara, cushioned between the mountains on one side and the ocean on the other. It is only because of plate tectonics that these mountains were pushed up millions of years ago and

I can now live in this wonderful scenery and climate that results from it. Anti-earthquakers, stop whining. You can't have it both ways!

Formulating a perhaps more precise concept of "evil" concerning the universe, it's when the universe gets in the way of my plans, or expectations. I didn't plan or expect my house to be swallowed by an earthquake, and the rude universe didn't heed my wishes! Don't get mad at the universe. That's easy to say, but when we apply it to the areas of say, cancer or death it becomes harder to understand. Yet, the same stills holds. Cancer is good. Why? Because life is good. Cells functioning are good. Cells mutating are good. It just happens that some of our bodies are in the way of the universe functioning, that is, certain types of cells doing their thing. Another example, polio. This phenomenon operates, and the phenomenon of polio vaccine operates as well. Both are good. The first phenomenon is only a disaster, humanly speaking, if we don't have access to the second. We are part of the natural functioning of the universe. That means we have a say in actually changing its course. So, of course we look for vaccines and cancer cures and mosquito repellants and perhaps some day even changing the nature of plate tectonics. The only thing that makes these "evil" is that they sometimes go against our plans and expectations.

This even applies to death. Most people consider death as evil, as the worst thing that could happen to them. (Editorial comment: The worst thing that could happen is people not living life while we have it!) But here's another way of looking at death: Emmanuel, a channeled being, says, "Death is very safe." If death is safe, what isn't?? In fact, if we didn't have death, think of what a disaster that would be! If every plant and bug and animal and person who ever lived were still living, this would not be a pleasant place! Even if only humans lived forever, what kind of a world would we have? Have you considered the aging process? Think of the vast number of ancients who would be roaming the planet. We've got enough to worry about as it is, with all the baby boomers creeping toward retirement, let alone millions of decrepit people all around! So, how about if we lived for ever and didn't get old? (Wasn't that a good word I invented earlier – "omnivivacious"?) But then again we are just trying to reinvent the universe to fit our narrow, immediate desires. Nothing can retain its vitality unless it has an interchange with other things, and it can't have that interchange unless those things can die (like when you eat a carrot). We have to have death to have life. So, if you don't want death, what you are really saying is that you want to live outside of time. But, according to Einstein and common sense, you'd then have to live outside of space as well. In a deathless existence there can be no physicality. Virtually everything in the universe, from the big bang to the amoebae, functions in a process we humans describe as birth-growth-maturation-decay. It is inconceivable that we could have physicality outside of the birth-growth-maturation-decay process. OK, so how about if we could live, oops, I mean, <u>be</u> forever outside of time, space and physicality? Well, that's precisely why death is required. You have to step outside of physicality. If you want immortality, you have to want death! I know I said this in the chapter on **Death**, but it bears repeating.

In summary, the universe is all good, even when it doesn't cooperate with our plans or expectations. We are grateful for what is; what isn't doesn't take away from what is. What isn't, isn't evil. What's good is good.

Summary

We use good and evil in three ways. When we apply these words to the universe itself, everything that exists is good. As humans we sometimes look at things such as earthquakes or sickness or death as evil. Yet, they are simply part of how the universe necessarily functions. We call these things "evil." That is only because we do not take a broad enough view of the situation, or because the situation does not meet our expectations. The universe is unfolding as it should. This is good. It is good.

Chapter 20:

SIN AND EVIL

What is personal evil? What is sin?

In the last chapter I spoke about good and evil on a universal level. Now I want to speak about it on a personal level. Evil on a personal level is called sin. What most people mean by sin is "doing something bad." I personally do not like the word "sin" because it implies that not only was the thing you did bad, but you are bad as well for doing it. This, then, brings in guilt, etc. I would rather make the distinction that the thing you did may be bad, but you are still good. You just made a mistake. We are all good people who make mistakes. That is my working definition for sin: a mistake. On a more profound level, the process of natural selection is one of "mis-takes." The universe keeps trying many possibilities until one "takes." All the other tries were mis-takes!

How do "mistakes" work? Let's take lying, for example. Let's say you tell somebody you will go to a meeting when you have no intention of going. That is bad, but you are not. You are acting like a kid who hasn't grown up yet. You wouldn't call a toddler who spills her milk "bad." You would say that she's just growing up and does "imperfect" things. She is immature and just doesn't have the knowledge/skill to not do it. In the case of lying about a meeting, you are too immature to say "no" because you think it will hurt the other person's feelings or, more likely, they will be annoyed at you or not like you. When we "grow up" we see that people become even more annoyed at us and dislike us more so when we don't tell the truth, so we start telling the truth. We are ready to accept short term pain for long term good. Doing "evil" is pursuing seeming short term gain for long term pain.

Let's add another dimension. Sin is not just a mistake, but it is one that harms another. The question is: Why do good people do bad things? Bad things are simply (and only) things that hurt other people. People also do bad things to themselves – they mutilate themselves, get drunk, get hurt, even kill themselves. Why? That seems to get to the heart of the question, because I suspect they do these things to themselves out of the same causes that they do them to others. What are these causes? Very simply, hurt people hurt others. Abused children become abusive parents. If you were abused, or even if you felt you didn't get enough love as a child, you are on the defensive. If you have an aggressive nature you will attack people who seem to be attacking you. Or if you have a passive nature, you will do things to be liked by others, such as lie to or manipulate them. As we mature, we get a stronger and stronger self image – we come to like ourselves, even with our failings – and we come to be less defensive, more accepting and less hurtful to others as well. Those who don't mature sufficiently hurt others – and themselves.

On a more fundamental level we have, as babies, an all-consuming need for survival. We will do whatever it takes to survive. When our survival is threatened, even if only in our imagination, we will do whatever we can do within our current resources to survive, even if it means lying, stealing, cheating, killing – hurting others. By "current resources" I mean that we solve all problems using the data bank we have in our heads (or autonomous nervous system). Some people don't have adequate data banks of experience to draw from. They don't have arsenals, including: understanding their own feelings and where those feelings came from, understanding other people's feelings, being able to use speech to resolve conflict, and so on. So they respond inappropriately to situations, as a child would. In a normal maturing process, we learn more and more about how we, others and life works. We become more and more assured of our survival, and act more and more out of freedom rather than out of reaction to supposed or real threat. Further, some people have genetic characteristics that cause abnormal behavior. For example, my son has Attention Deficit Disorder. He does impulsive things, because he is like a hunter-gatherer trapped in an agricultural society. We are learning that depression may be a chemical flaw, not a character flaw. People whose parents had mental illness are themselves prone to it as well. We are not sure yet what comes from "nature or nurture," so that, as Paul says, "The good that I will, I do not; the evil that I would not, that I do." (Sorry about the language; I haven't looked at new *Bible* translations lately.) So, behaviors may be genetic (nature), or they may come out of faulty upbringing (nurture). Going back, the parents' behavior come out of nature or nurture as well, and on and on: "The sins of the fathers are visited upon the children."

Why do good people do bad things?

To summarize, here are four reasons people hurt others:

1. Immature knowledge/skill – we just don't know any better, or know how to respond any better. We are children on the way to being adults.

2. Immature self-image – we don't like ourselves or don't feel good about ourselves. So we will do things to try to be liked or respected by others, or to try to "force" them to like us.

3. Immature self-defense system – we do inappropriate things because we think they will aid our survival when we feel threatened, either physically or psychologically.

4. Not recognizing and handling our compulsions or uncontrollable emotions – We don't take steps to get outside help to gain control over behaviors that seem

to control us because of genetic causes or deficient upbringing.

All of these sources of "sin" – people hurting others – do not take place on the rational level. They are sub- or pre- or un- rational. We're all just at different stages of development. The process of human growth is to bring the rational, the reflective, to bear on the non-reflective. We are all someplace along the growth continuum. Unfortunately, some of us get stuck at a particular place and are not able to move on.

This is not to say that people aren't responsible when they do bad things. They <u>are</u> responsible; they are just not culpable. Responsibility means: I did a bad thing whether I admit it or not, i.e. – somebody got hurt as a result of my agency (not like an insurance agency; "agency" is just a fancy word for "act"). When we "take responsibility" we admit: I did it, I see the bad consequences of doing it (somebody being hurt), I wish it didn't happen, and I'm willing to repair things if I can. Culpability implies guilt. That means I did it and I am a bad person for it.

What if somebody admits responsibility for bad behavior but keeps doing it anyhow, like a drunk who harms his or her family? Responsibility also means recognizing that you are trapped by a compulsion and that you need help from others to manage the compulsion – like going to a therapist, Alcoholics Anonymous, etc. It's not our fault that we are an alcoholic, but we are absolutely responsible for getting control over it. Am I doing away with guilt? I'd like to. I'm not doing away with sorrow or remorse. But, to me, guilt adds the dimension, "I am a bad person for it."

Punishment

This brings us to the idea of "punishment." Should people be punished to see the consequences of their action when they hurt someone? I don't think so. When my toddler poops in her pants, she doesn't have to be told that this isn't a good thing to do. Spanking her won't make any positive difference. When we poop on another or the planet, we know that this was not a good thing to do. (Let me distinguish between real poop and metaphorical poop: real poop, judiciously disposed of, is usually very good for the planet.) When somebody doesn't see that what they did hurt someone, show them. If the person is an adult, and showing them the consequences doesn't change their behavior, he or she is trapped in a level of immaturity which requires psychological counseling or other help to get untrapped.

Should society, then, not punish criminals? Society should help rehabilitate the immature people who commit crimes, just as parents help their children to grow to their next level of maturity. The only purpose of punishment, other than vindictiveness, is to change the future for the better. Unfortunately, our "houses of correction" are doing just the opposite to people – they are fixing them into patterns that are destructive to themselves and society. I am not saying that we should get rid of jails. We need to protect ourselves. If people consistently hurt others, they ought to be locked up. But that is not for their sake; it is for ours. They should be rehabilitated as well. Unfortunately, our prison system makes little distinction between those who are mentally ill and those who aren't, between addicts and non-addicts, between the violent and non-violent, between victim-less and victim crimes. It is a vindictive, destructive system. It is based on the fallacy that there are good people and bad people; if you are in jail you are de facto bad, and if you are outside, you are good. Perhaps we should have three distinct types of jails:

1. Incarceration centers for the violent.
2. Rehabilitation centers for the mentally ill and the addicted.
3. Rehabilitation centers for non-violent criminals.

Of course, the more effective # 2 is, the less need we would have for #1. I am compelled to add one more point. I understand that the majority of prisoners have learning disorders or ADHD. Perhaps our school system was the first prison they were in, because it failed to identify them, give them alternate learning and made them "bad and wrong," rather than an esteemed learner!

To summarize some distinctions about "punishment":

1. People should be shown they've hurt somebody or something, if they don't clearly recognize it. Children periodically need to be "grounded" or need a "time out" to help them get clearer vision.
2. If they <u>do</u> see it's wrong, but still can't seem to stop doing it, they need help. This applies to both children and adults. The help may be on the physical level: for example, Ritalin for an ADHD child, or estrogen for menopausal women, or laxatives for men, or what-ever medication schizophrenics take, and so on. Or it may be on the psychological level of psychotherapy, twelve-step programs, pastoral counseling, and so on.
3. They should repair the damage they have done.
4. If they do violent things to others, they should be locked up for <u>our</u> protection – until we are clear that they will not do them again.

I have been talking about sins of commission. The same principle applies to sins of omission: we are responsible. But don't get hung up on this. We "omit" constantly. As I edit this about 27,000 people die every day from prevent-able malnutrition and disease. What have you done today to stop this? There is always more we can do to better the lives of others and ourselves. Don't worry about all of it; just do what's next for you now. If you don't do anything for others now, it's because you're feeling insecure or bad about yourself. Take care of yourself first. Get the help you need. Love yourself; then you can take care of others. But if days and weeks and months and years go by and you still haven't gotten to helping others because you are still helping yourself, then the way to help yourself is to help others now.

How about sinning against the planet? When we hurt the planet, we are ultimately hurting others. On a deeper level you could say that we should treat everything in the universe according to its nature. Throwing rocks is okay; throwing cats is not. Everything that exists is sacred, each according to its own level.

Perhaps the final caveat is: Don't worry about the sins of others, worry about your own. Be wise and protect yourself, but be patient with the immature hordes out there. Also, don't even worry about your own sins. Acknowledge when something you did hurt someone (or yourself), make restitution if appropriate and ask for and give forgiveness. Acknowledge your goodness and move on.

Summary

Personal evil, or sin, is the mistake of hurting others. There are four reasons people hurt others. Some of them are inter-related:

1. Immature knowledge/skill – we just don't know any better, or know how to respond any better. We are children on the way to being adults.
2. Immature self-image – we don't like ourselves or don't feel totally good about ourselves. So we will do things to try to be liked or respected by others, or to try to "force" them to like us.
3. Immature self-defense system – we do inappropriate things because we think they will aid our survival when we feel threatened, either physically or psychologically.
4. Not recognizing and handling our compulsions or uncontrolled emotions – we don't take steps to get outside help to gain control over behaviors that seem to control us because of genetic causes or deficient upbringing.

Doing bad things does not mean that we are bad. It means that we are immature – stuck somewhere in the continuum of growth, and needing to take our next step forward. Punishment doesn't seem to work very well.

Chapter 21:
PRAYER

What is prayer?

As with other re-definitions in this book, I define prayer in a way that is positive and useful to me. Prayer is the natural act of reflection. Reflection etymologically means "bending back." Although other animals know, humans seem to be the ones who know that they know, who can bend back and watch themselves knowing. Another way to say this is that we have self-consciousness. Prayer could be said to be the act of doing this. A Jesuit I once read said, "Experience without reflection is not educative; it is just one damn thing after another." Prayer is when you stop doing, in order to think about the doing (without falling asleep).

This moves away from the traditional kinds of prayer, which I learned long ago: adoration, thanksgiving, petition and contrition. These are somewhat useful categories, but as you would expect, I am going to reinterpret them here.

First, adoration/worship. As I said earlier, god doesn't need that stuff. If he's the big guy we think he is, he doesn't really need us to say, "Hey, wow, you're a Big Guy! We're not!" Adoration may important to us as human beings if it helps us to pull back from daily life and see with awe the majesty of the universe, and to see both the grandeur and smallness of our own individual place in it. If it helps to bring a god into the picture, go for it. It is just that she is not personally attached to being brought in.

The same thing goes for prayer of thanksgiving: god doesn't need it, we may. Thanksgiving is another way of recognizing how great and graced our presence here is, and the presence of all things in the universe. It flows naturally from adoration. But, how can you be thankful if there's nobody out there to thank? If there is somebody out there, and you are being thankful, she'll get it. If there isn't anybody out there, thankfulness is still useful for two reasons: First, it is a recognition of the way things are in the universe – that everything is pure gift. Secondly, if we really are thankful, then the natural extension of that is to share, give to others, what we have received. So, de facto, when we are sharing with others, that in itself is a prayer of thanksgiving.

Concerning the third type of prayer, petition, even if a god did exist as a person who could answer prayers, he wouldn't bend the laws of the universe to answer somebody's prayer. Things work the way they work. If it is going to rain on Saturday, it is going to rain on Saturday, and praying like hell won't make any difference. Some prayers are answered but not outside the bounds of how things normally work. Let's say rain was forecast, and you prayed for it not to happen. Then, a south wind came up and it didn't rain. It just happened that the way things normally work corresponded to what your wishes were. That wind was going to come up whether you asked for it or not. Imagine if the Democrats said, "Oh god, let us win," and the Republicans said, "Oh god, let us win," who's prayers would he answer? He'd probably say, "Oh god, nobody wins." (Sorry, I had to throw that in.)

Prayers of petition do have value, but the value is again for us. They help us to get very clear about what we want, what our goals are, what we are striving to accomplish. Then, they may set us in motion to take those steps within our power to achieve our goals. Or they put us intuitively on the lookout for those things that will help us reach our desires. The most enlightened and powerful prayer of petition is: "Oh god, let be what is."

The same thing goes for contrition: god doesn't need it; we may. If you have done something wrong, you should recognize it, which is different from feeling sorry. You should feel sorry if you feel sorry, and should not feel sorry if you don't feel sorry. ("Oh god, let be what is.") However, if something you did didn't work, you need to recognize that it didn't work, period. As I said in the last chapter, you don't have to make yourself a bad guy for it. You just need to say: What I did, didn't work and here's why (if you can see why). Also, obviously, if you hurt someone else, apologize and make up for it. That is the real value of contrition: You recognize what didn't work and make up for it appropriately. Putting god in creates a middle man. If I sock you, I need to apologize to you, not to god and then you.

Getting back to prayer as a form of reflection, this is what meditation is. When you're meditating you are either thinking about something, being acutely present to something, or simply having an awareness of being. In one sense, "thinking about something," is something we're doing all day long. But I distinguish between actively trying to think about things – which seems to be a left brain activity – and "watching the movies of your mind" – which is a right brain activity. As I see it, meditation is actually a higher form of daydreaming. Daydreaming usually implies that your mind is flitting around. Mediation is more focused, peaceful concentration. But it is not trying to focus; it is allowing the focus to happen. So it is being in the presence of something, some thought; or it is an awareness of being itself. Every thought we have is a gift from the universe; it just shows up. And sometimes after daydreaming a while, better, more exhilarating, more awesome thoughts show up. It is at those times that I more clearly get in touch with the awesome graciousness of the universe.

What is the difference between meditation and contemplation? I'm not sure of the distinction between them or whether there is a distinction. My working definition of contemplation is: it is the awareness of or being present to being. It is simply – and profoundly – the recognition that the universe, in whatever particular aspect of its splendor we are recognizing, exists. And that we ourselves exist; that we are, rather than are not.

I must say that I do not do very much meditation or contemplation. I am not very successful at it. There are many profound and wise teachers who actually are. However, although I don't do a lot of silent meditation, I do a lot of free-flow writing. I consider this as another form of meditation. In thinking or writing – whatever way we have of reflecting – communication is the essential element in it. We can communicate with ourselves, or others, or the universe. If bringing in "god" – whatever your picture of her is – enables you to communicate, then go for it. I have found that there doesn't have to be a receiver of the communication for it to be useful. Perhaps a better way of saying that is that I receive my own communication. I am both the deliverer and the receiver!

Summary

Prayer is the natural act of reflection. The traditional kinds of prayer are: adoration, thanksgiving, petition, contrition. These are ways which help us reflect on, or communicate to ourselves, about the universe. They are useful for our own benefit; but an outie god has no vested interest in or need for them.

Chapter 22:

THE FUTURE AND THE PRESENT

A Brief Mystery of Time – Part 1

Can god tell the future? Can anyone tell the future? What is the future?

Neither god, nor anybody else, can tell the future. To repeat some ideas I shared in the chapter **God – Other Possibilities**, Alan Watts says that if god knew the future she would get so bored that she would invent randomness just to make it interesting for herself. So, god created a game for herself whereby she is just as in the dark about the future as we are. This leads us to the realization that to know the future is a contradiction in terms. For example, if you knew you were to be hit by a car while crossing a particular street today, you would just avoid crossing that street. Then you wouldn't be hit by the car, so you didn't know the future! If we knew things within our control would turn out badly, we would change them. So, by definition, we can't know the future. If you knew it, it wouldn't be the future but the present.

Further, if we knew who was going to win a football game, or that on the third pitch the batter was going to line out to the third baseman, we wouldn't go to the game. Well, maybe we would, as we would go to a play or movie more than once. Then we say, "Look, look; he's going to line out to the third baseman." But in general, if we knew the future, life would be very boring. So, to make it interesting we, along with god, don't know and don't want to know the future.

In a sense we do know the future inasmuch as certain events happen regularly. The sun will rise tomorrow. If we drop a cup it will fall. We know the "laws of the universe." We come to discover regularity (from the Latin "regula" – "rule") of the universe and then conduct ourselves accordingly. We can't know the results of randomness, otherwise it wouldn't be random. Once we get to discover when something isn't random but regular – like every time I put my hand in a fire it burns – then we can use and build on that knowledge and move on to the next level of randomness. The process of discovery is just that – seeing how the universe operates, seeing order in what was previously thought of as chaos or randomness – and making use of that knowledge.

If we came to a point where everything necessary was known, and all our needs were taken care of because of this knowledge, then we would invent games like golf and all the thousands of games we are inventing now, precisely because we demand randomness in our lives. Can you imagine playing golf and knowing what your score was going to be ahead of time? If people knew, that surely would ruin a good game, and an industry!

Life is a Game

This brings us to the wonderful theory that all of life is a game. What is a game? It is an activity where we expend energy to pursue an arbitrary goal by following certain rules we invent. A game has no meaning outside of itself and is played solely for the purpose of enjoyment. Yet, isn't that a great description of life itself? Life has no meaning outside itself; once the game is over, it is over. We invent goals and rules for ourselves so that we can enjoy the game, enjoy life. The only purpose of the game is to enjoy it. Not knowing the future is what makes it such a wonderful game. We/god are playing this game of not knowing how things are going to end up. So, enjoy the game. That's what games are for!

Another way of looking at the future is to realize that there is no such thing as the future. The future is just a construct in our minds. All that exists is the present. What is real is what is now. Of course, the thoughts and hopes and plans that go on in our heads or that we have captured on paper or computer are real, but they are only real as thoughts and hopes. I am not downplaying the value of hopes and plans. In fact, I love the two thoughts:

- Everything you do or have was an idea first.
- Everything gets created twice.

The future is very real in our thoughts, hopes, plans, but that is the only place it has reality – in our heads. It only exists as the thought I am having now. When the next thought comes, the last thought no longer has a reality, although it may be stored in our memory bank. Life is a succession of "now's," each real in successive instants. A conclusion is that no one can know the future because it isn't real, it doesn't exist.

Summary

Not knowing the future is what gives joy and excitement to life. If a god did know the future, she would invent randomness just to make things interesting for herself. If we knew how things would turn, we could change them. If we changed them, de facto we didn't know the future. By definition, we can't know the future. Another way of saying this is that there is no such thing as the future. Only the present exists.

Chapter 23:

THE PAST

A Brief Mystery of Time – Part 2

Does the past exist?

Since I just wrote about the future, I thought I would put in a few thoughts about the past. Does the past exist? Most people would say yes. But if you ask where it exists, the answer is, as with the future: only in people's minds. You might say it exists in history books or artifacts, but then they only have meaning if there is a human mind to interpret them. You also might say that it exists in our genetic code or our upbringing. But my answer to that is that although the past has shaped the present, none of it exists any more. All that exists is the present. The me that is shaped by the past exists, but not the past. The past, just as the future, is very real, by the way, but that reality exists only in our heads.

What is the significance of this? It means that at any or every moment in time we get to create a new present for ourselves. It means that we are not bound by the past. At any moment we can change our behavior, even though we have acted a certain way for fifty years. Every day, every moment is the opportunity for a new beginning. Even though we are creatures of habit, we don't have to be bound by the habit. We can change the habit. The past may have a strong grip on us (in other words, we have strong habits of thought or action), yet it doesn't necessarily determine the future. The way I like to say this is: The past doesn't determine the future except by default. In other words, we do continue to live our past patterns unless we make a conscious decision to change. The past way of action is the default mode we fall into if we don't make a change.

I love the game of golf because it is a miniature version of the game of life. The key question in both games is: how fast can you recover? Recovering means that we are willing to give up the past and to live in the present. With every shot you have the opportunity to start anew and not dwell on the last shot, which after all doesn't exist except in your head (and on the scorecard). Even if you hit 10 poor shots in a row, you have the capability of hitting a great one now. Life is the same. It only exists in the present, in the succession of now, now, now, now. At every moment we have the opportunity of dropping the past and creating a new present, a new now.

How is that for a short chapter? I talked about the future, so I wanted to say something about the past. But more than that, I wanted to draw a picture of what it truly means to be human – and divine. That is, we get to be creators of our own life at every moment. This leads to the next chapters, **God's Will** and **The Meaning of Life**.

Summary

Don't be lazy. There are only five paragraphs in this chapter. Read them!

Chapter 24:

GOD'S WILL

How can one discover god's will?

When we use the phrase "god's will" we usually are thinking of one of three things:

> 1. How we should conduct our lives, morally speaking.
> 2. What we should do with our lives – i.e., what goals, purpose we should have
> 3. How the whole universe does or should operate – the divine plan.

Since I have discussed #1, morality, already, let's look at the second and third possibilities. Both of these presume a plan, a way things will or must turn out – in my life and in the universe. Yet, as I just wrote, there can be no such thing as knowing the future. Another way to say this is that there are generally two ways to discover what "should be": before things happen or after things happen. We can only know what "should be" in the second way – after things happen.

If there is a god and she has something she wants you to do with your life, you can't know what that is beforehand. Let's say you thought god wanted you to be an accountant and you became one, that would be god's will. Let's say you thought god didn't want you to be an accountant and you became one anyway, then that would be god's will. Or, let's say you didn't care one way or the other about what god

155

wanted, and you became an accountant, then that would be god's will. If there were an omnipotent god out there who had a plan, there is no way we could <u>not</u> do exactly what she wants. So, it is foolish to even think about it.

Similarly, we can't know god's will for the whole universe before things happen because god can't even know it. If there were a god, she couldn't know the future, because that is self-contradictory as I just discussed. People who claim they know god's will ahead of time, like all the predictors of the end of the world, or Jim Jones in Guyana, or David Koresh in Waco, or the Heavenly Gate gang, can enroll people to do some crazy things. These are far out examples of people who claimed to know "god's will." What about really holy people who say they know? Yet, how do we know who is really holy? Whom do you follow? The odds are you will follow a guy or gal because they live down the street, or because they live in India, or because your brother-in-law heard about somebody, or you were channel-surfing and saw some guy on television. How do you know there's not a guy in Brazil who <u>really</u> knows. You haven't done exhaustive research, so how do you know the guy you picked or the one your mom picked is the right one?

What if you decide to follow someone who you think is a very good person? That certainly is a more valid way to decide whom to follow than following certain TV evangelists. But, as I discussed in the chapter on **Revelation**, when you follow someone you are using your judgment to select someone to whom you will now give up your judgment. So, why not just stick to your own judgment all the time? In fact, when you judge the validity of what someone has to say, you <u>are</u> using your own judgment, so you really think that <u>you</u> know god's will. The only plausible way to understand god's will is this: god's will is for you to use your judgment to live your life the way you think it should be lived, and to follow others only inasmuch as what they say makes sense to you.

Concerning the third meaning for "the will of god," – a plan for how the universe does or should operate – is there a divine plan? A plan means there is a pre-ordained path. In one sense there does seem to be a plan. There seems to be a forward thrust in the universe which I spoke of earlier, and which has definitely made me, us, its beneficiaries. But in another sense, looking at how the universe seems to have been operating for the pasts 12 billion years, the operating principle has been random selection.

I am profoundly influenced by Carl Sagan and Ann Druyan's book, *Shadows of Forgotten Ancestors*. It is almost a foundation for my theological beliefs. In brief, what I get out of it is that everything got here by chance, by random selection, not by some divine, inexorable plan. Or, another way you could say it is that the divine plan is random selection, or, evolution. That is, the universe continually throws out trillions of random or chance events. Then, survival of the fittest takes over – smaller celestial bodies get sucked up by bigger ones. Alpha males beat up beta males. The "fittest" wins. But it is not a question of "winning." It is just a question of what works better. If you are a giraffe whose neck just happens to be longer, you reach the taller leaves and you are healthier than others. You have more kids than others. Your kids are healthier, and your genes have a better chance at surviving and being passed on. Perhaps there is an overall plan that man, we, should be at the end of the process. We have the capacity to stand back and see the process operating: we know. Because we have knowledge, we can start to manage this randomness and shape the planet and perhaps some day the rest of the universe. If human freedom is part of the plan, there can really be no specific "end result" in the plan. In the final analysis, then, whether there is a plan or not really doesn't matter. Nobody can really know for sure, at least until we are out of this cosmos.

Looking at how the world unfolds, we can take two points of view. First, the universe is incredibly abundant. For example, my peach tree produces hundreds of peaches every year. Just one peach pit grew into a plant that reproduces thousands of times over in its lifetime. The second point of view is that the universe is incredibly stupid and wasteful. Thousands and thousands of peaches are produced, just in the hope that one of them will germinate, take root and produce another peach tree. Who planned this anyhow? Couldn't she have done any better?

But that last thought signals something about the nature of the universe, and the nature of man. That is, knowing is all-important. As I discussed in the chapter on **The Future and the Present**, if we knew what the plan was, we could then alter the plan. Therefore there would be no plan. Bill Murray said in *Groundhog Day*, "Perhaps god isn't omnipotent; perhaps he just knows everything." So, knowing gives us the ability to alter what happens. As humans, we have the ability to alter the future. Bill knew that little boy would fall out of the tree, so he went and caught him. He altered the future. He participated in and changed the Divine plan. Bill was divine! (Andee McDowall was more so!)

Someone having the old outie concept of god might say: "Yes, but god knew that Bill would know, so part of the divine plan was to have Bill come to know and therefore to alter the plan. And that is really part of the overall, bigger plan." But what if Bill knew that, and he decided "The hell with it: I'll show god; I'll just let the damn kid fall!" Then outie-ists would say: "Yes, but god knew Bill would rebel, so he wanted Bill to know and to purposely not do something, which would mean the kid would fall after all, which is exactly what I want (for my own inscrutable reasons)!" Do you see how maddening this line of reasoning is? It is a form of circular lose-lose reasoning.

A better way to look at it: Perhaps not only Bill and Andee are god, but perhaps we are all god. Perhaps precisely because we do know, we can and do alter the future. We actually create it. We actually decide on and carry out the plan! We don't go out and gather random ears of corn in the wild. We know how corn works, so we plant it for our benefit. We are masters of the garden. Accepting our divine nature, we have the opportunity to create the world as we want it. I was going to say "the responsibility," but we are responsible to no one but ourselves. The only ones who are going to say what's right and wrong about what we do is us. We get to participate, really, in the act of creation. We get to bring something into being which would not be if we didn't do it. What we choose to bring into being, is what gets created.

As Barbara Marx Hubbard says, we participate in "Conscious Evolution." We are responsible for the next level of evolution: Chance brought us to this point; choice brings us the future. The way things are is the plan; natural selection is the way things "should" be. This will become clearer when you read the chapter on **The Meaning of Life**. How else could the universe be except the way that it is? The best I can say is what the Desiderata prayer says: "The universe is unfolding itself as it should." When we know what causes smallpox we can – and did – change it. Part of the universe unfolding itself is us doing some of the unfolding. That's the divine plan.

Summary

There is no pre-ordained "god's will." Nobody can discover what should be before things happen, only after they happen. If there is a plan, we can't know it. If we can know it, and thus alter it, it wasn't a plan! The way things are is the plan: random natural selection is the way things "should have been" to this point. Conscious evolution is the way it "should be" now.

There are no "shoulds" in life. (My former business partner Brian used to say, "Don't 'should' on me!") If there is a god outside of this universe, she wants us to be responsible for making up what his or her will should be.

Chapter 25:

THE MEANING OF LIFE

What is the meaning of life?

The shortest answer I can give to the question is: the meaning of life is to create the meaning of life. There are two basic approaches to understanding the idea of "meaning." In tandem to what I just said about god's will in the last chapter, the first, is to presume that there is some meaning out there which we are to discover. If there were a meaning out there, how are we to discover it? It has to be interpreted and expressed through people. If we discover it within ourselves, how do we know that we are not deluding ourselves? Whom should we believe? How would we know who has the right meaning? The second approach is to presume that there is no preordained meaning to life and that we get to create the meaning we choose. I side with theory number two. There are a certain set of givens: We are here, we breathe, we see, we move, etc. We are free to make whatever meaning we want out of this set of givens and to choose our own path among them.

Some people may think this is bad news. I think it is great news! If we understand the word "god" as the Grand Metaphor, this creates some awesome possibilities. If "god" attests to the joy, wonder and awesomeness of life – of this freely-given, ever-evolving piece of time/space in which we have the opportunity to create our lives – that means that all being is sacred because we participate in the motion/energy/life force of the universe. To the extent that we share in being, we are all godly. We are part of creation, not only as created but as creators. That means beings with intelligence get to create, to invent, the meaning of life. We get to be in charge of the universe, or at least our piece of it. The universe does not make sense, has absolutely no meaning, unless we say so. It is in our power to create meaning through what we say and what we do. If we say the universe has meaning or if we say it doesn't, we are right. We are little co-creators of the universe. Meaning comes about simply because we say so: "By the word were all things made."

Of course, as I said earlier, there could be a god outside of all this, and an extrinsic meaning to all of this. But that is beyond our power to know. If there were an all-powerful god and some extrinsic meaning to life, it would be impossible for us not to fulfill it anyhow. Also, if there were an extrinsic meaning, what could it be: Place all the petunia petals in the world on the Rock of Gibraltar? How far different could god's meaning be than what the most enlightened of mankind have been saying for ages anyhow: Be truthful, be peaceful, love one another, respect the earth, share, etc.? So the way things look now, the quality of godliness exists only in and through us, in and through the universe. If we don't end wars, if we don't end hunger, if we don't end environmental degradation, then of course the universe is not benign, doesn't make sense. So, if we don't act intelligently, lovingly, forward-thrustingly, then in truth, there is "no god." In other words, we may not have started all this, but we get to finish it, our little terrestrial piece of it anyhow.

What does "meaning" mean?

Talking about this brings up a more fundamental question: What does "meaning" mean? The best answer I can come up with for now is: It is a story we make up about given phenomena that relate them to other phenomena. Take a baseball game for instance. A person hits a ball with a stick and runs to a base and then to another base and another base and back to where he started from. What does this mean? There are several answers. On the level of phenomena you can say it doesn't mean anything. It means a person hit a ball with a stick and ran to three bases and back to where he started. On another level, though, it means our team scored a run. What does that mean? It means we win the game. And what does that mean? It means we win the World Series. And what does that mean? It means that we are the world champions. And what does that mean? It means that our city is the greatest. What does that mean? Basically nothing. But it is a good story we make up because it makes us feel good. Real life is the same way. We "give" meaning to things. We make up stories that relate a series of things together, which sounds plausible and which makes us feel good – or bad.

Asking "what is the point?" when another is communicating is another way of asking "what does this mean?" We are searching for how what is now being said relates to what was said previously: How do all of the things you are saying relate to each other? Ultimately, how does this relate to me? For example, I say, "the Jones kids are coming home from school early." Response: So what? I.e., no meaning here; it doesn't relate to me. Now, if I happen to be Mr. Jones, I might say: "Hey, we can go to the beach" (positive effect on me), or, possibly, "Oh nuts, now I won't be able to get my work done" (negative effect). Meaning means that I can relate any given data to myself in a positive, negative or neutral way.

This discussion reverts back to what I said in the chapter on **Truth**. Reality is composed of two things:

1. Phenomena: data, facts, what happens, and,
2. What we make of these facts, or how we interpret them, or the meaning that we create out of them.

Meaning is the belief or story we make up about something; the meaning of life is the story we make up about life.

It is not trivial that I used baseball as an example above. Is there a fundamental difference between the game of baseball and the game of life? I don't think so. We show up here as babies, we grow up, we get married, we have kids, we die. Going into the grave is just like going around the bases to home plate in a baseball game. It is over, and what did it mean? It means whatever we made it to mean while it was happening. To say that life is a game might seem to trivialize it. But life isn't <u>merely</u> a game; it is a great, glorious, grand, and wonderful game. People have a lot of fun at baseball games, and we can have a lot of fun in life, if we choose to. Unfortunately, a lot of the time we are sitting in a baseball park waiting for a football game to begin!

If you find some resistance to what I am saying about the meaning of life, how about this as an alternative: Kurt Vonnegut tells the story about an inter-galactic war where one of the space ships had to land at an obscure outpost planet which happened to be called Earth. It required a special screw to repair the space ship and this screw happened to be from an old Ford or something, which was lying rusting right where the spaceship landed. So the crew used the screw and continued its journey. The whole purpose of the earth was to have created a civilization that eventually produced cars which eventually produced this Ford that happened to have this screw which was at the right spot for the spaceship when it landed. That was the entire purpose for the existence of the earth and humans. Not a very happy-ending, right? Perhaps it is not that far from the truth. There are billions of galaxies with billions of stars which have billions of planets. Who knows what the purpose of this outpost planet is, or my outpost life in this outpost expansion of the big bang oscillation world series?

Kurt Vonnegut made up a story, which doesn't mean anything unless we give meaning to it. If there is a correct story, a correct meaning to life imposed from without, we are not going to find out about it until we die. Then it is too late. The alternative is to live life as if you have the opportunity to create whatever you want out of it. We can invent stories or meanings that empower us, make us feel good, make us do good things, make our lives zestful.

I mentioned earlier that perhaps humor is the fundamental response to life. That ties in with the idea of life being a game. We are trapped between the two great poles of human existence. We get to be in charge of the universe and direct it in our own little way. How magnificent: if it is to be, I create it. I, we, are in charge of where the universe is going. The other pole is: we have no say whatsoever. Man proposes, but god, the universe disposes. Man plans; god laughs. We make our plans and play our little games and the universe says: Sorry, not this time. An earthquake says "You're out of here, you are gone." So, what is the appropriate attitude toward this? It is laughter. Laughter is the admission: "I thought I was in charge here, but I'm not!" It is the constant willingness to let go, to get back into the flow of the universe, and to make some more plans!

Frank's Meaning of Life

What is the meaning that I have personally created out of life? It is that we are here to have a good time and to help others have a good time. Is this profound or what? Actually, I think it is very profound. Life is a game. A game is a set of activities people agree to which has no purpose or meaning other than the enjoyment of the set of activities. That is my interpretation of what life is about. It is a combination of "Eat, drink and be merry," and what Jesus said: "Feed the hungry, clothe the naked, etc." Enjoy the goods of the earth yourself, and make sure everybody else does too.

Of course, there are negative interpretations of the meaning of life: "Life is hard; then you die;" or "Most of us are condemned to lead lives of quiet desperation." On the one hand, people who actually feel like this are probably in a lot of pain, and I have sympathy for them. On the other hand, I would tell them to get a life. Read the section on victimhood in my book *Don't Go To Work Unless It's Fun!* Or, just read on to the next chapter in this book, **Happiness**.

Some people might find depressing the idea that we get to create our own meaning in life and that life is a game. Actually it should be exhilarating. When I say there is no meaning except the meaning we create, this points to our divinity – the power, glory and grandeur of man. We get to be co-creators of the universe. If we decide to blow ourselves up, then that's how the story ends. If we decide to create a magnificent non-profit corporation of six billion well-paid members, then that's how the movie ends. We all get to write the script! What a treat!

We get to play the role of god, to create a world and meaning in the world for no other reason than we choose to. When Lawrence of Arabia was asked to justify an action, he said: "Because it pleases me." Or, an ex-monk friend of mine was asked by his religious superior to think carefully for two weeks about why he was leaving the monks, which he did. The answer he gave to the superior was: "Because I <u>want</u> to." My word, my saying so, invents the reality. If you are going to make up a story about life (or if you are going to buy into a story someone else made up), make sure it is a good one, a big enough one. Consider joining me in creating that all-inclusive non-profit corporation of six billion well-paid individuals (six billion in 1999; the number will go up!). There are a lot of job openings for Co-founders!

As I review this, I see that several ideas in this chapter are similar to those in the last chapter. I hope the nuances in meaning have been useful.

Summary

There is no pre-ordained meaning to life. Even if there were, who knows what it is? Whom should we listen to? We each get to determine the meaning of our own life, and, collectively, of all human life. Life is a game and we are here to enjoy ourselves during the game. Of course, I can't enjoy myself if someone next to me is suffering, so that means that we are all here to enjoy ourselves collectively. Since we can know and can shape the universe, let's do it magnificently, for god's sake! That is the meaning of life.

Chapter 26:

HAPPINESS– WHAT IS IT?

What is happiness?

Some would say that if you have to ask, you don't have it. It is a state of being that "feels good." But that applies to many levels. There are at least six different levels of happiness that I can think of, six areas in which we use the word. They are:

1. physical well-being
2. fun and pleasure
3. security
4. peace or contentment
5. joy
6. fulfilled expectations.

When we use the word happiness we could be referring to any of these states. These six levels are similar to Abraham Maslow's hierarchy of being, only in reverse order. As Maslow says, when you seem to achieve one, you look for the next. So let's look at each.

1. Physical happiness

Physical happiness works in two ways: absence of pain or

presence of pleasure. These are two distinct situations. What is the opposite of happy? Sad. If you are not happy, does that mean you are sad? Not necessarily. There is a whole neutral area of being neither sad nor happy. When you are in pain, illness, discomfort, dis-ease, then happiness means healing yourself, taking care of yourself, returning to the state of physical well-being — health. Once you are in the state of well-being, you are in a neutral state. It looked like a very positive state when you were unhealthy, but once you get there you soon consider it neutral. You begin to think of positive things to do that will bring pleasure. There are a multitude of things we do that can bring pleasure, which I will talk about briefly in # 2 below.

That being said, I still see physical well-being as an elevated state of happiness. As the old saying goes, "As long as you have your health . . . ." I say this for two reasons. First, when people are unhappy, it's often because of a physical problem: They are sick, they are in pain, they are sore, they are uncomfortable. But when those things are gone, they feel fine. They are now happily unaware of the unhappiness that used to be. The second reason is from my own experience. As I go through life, I find that more and more of what I thought were psychological problems, were actually physical problems. 99% of my "problems" really could boil down to: I'm tired, I'm hungry, I'm tense, I have chemical imbalances or toxins in my body, or I'm constipated. If you are unhappy it always pays to check out the physical first.

2. Fun or pleasure

Ideally, all of us would spend every day eating great food, having sex, winning at black jack, lowering our golf handicap, etc. Doing pleasurable things is wonderful, but pursuing these things alone is not the path to happiness — or at least not my path to happiness. If we over-pursue one pleasurable thing, there are negative consequences. Eating too much gives you indigestion, makes you fat, makes you indolent, etc. Too much golf starts to become painful, physically, psychologically or financially. Moderation is not a negative. It means to maximize our overall pleasure, to enjoy as fully as we can all the pleasures of life in balance – physical, psychological, intellectual, social, etc. It is certainly a laudable goal to move toward consistently having fun. (Remember my fantasy of heaven?) The hard part to remember is that fun is fun as long as it is fun. You are, again, the arbiter. Sometimes we pretend that what used to be fun is still fun – maybe it's time to sell the boat. Admitting this brings us to open ourselves to the next broader level of happiness.

3. Security

Security is a form of psychological happiness. It means, "I know I'm okay and that I can take care of my needs not only today but tomorrow as well." More precisely, it is the sense in a child, "I will be taken care of," and in an adult, "I can take care of myself and my loved ones. I have resources both inside of and outside of myself." This sense of security does not come from our circumstances or surroundings; it comes from an internal decision. There are still some 400,000 hunter-gatherers on the planet today. Some are secure and say: "We will find enough food today." On the other hand, there are some $100,000-per- year professionals who say: "I don't know what I'd do if I lost my job." My sense is that there is more security among the hunter-gatherers than the $100,000 professionals.

For many people, trust in god has provided a sense of security. I would re-interpret that and say "a trust in the benevolence of the universe." That includes a trust in one's self: "I am capable; I can find or create what I need. The universe wouldn't have put me here unless it gave me the capability of functioning within it." How does one find this trust in the universe and in one's self? You don't find it; you declare it. That's what I meant when I said that security is an internal decision. This is the magnificence of what it means to be human. We get to create our own lives by saying so. To make this choice, it helps if we were raised by loving parents in a secure atmosphere. But what if you weren't? What are you going to do, pine away the rest of your life? You make the choice anyhow – and have the courage to take the appropriate actions.

4. Peace or contentment

Peace is a deeper form of happiness which includes not only feeling good about physical well-being and security, but also the idea of contentment: All is well with the world. There is, of course, the possibility of self-delusion concerning peace and security. The world may be falling down around someone, and he fools himself by saying that everything's fine. Yet, if we step back, we all fool ourselves every day by saying everything's fine, when it isn't. The process of maturity is opening ourselves more and more to the world around us. To survive we have to shut out most of reality. If we personally witnessed each day even <u>one</u> of the 27,000 people (at this editing) who die every day from malnutrition and preventable causes, we would go crazy. So, to survive, we shut things out. We don't think about it, or even allow ourselves to perceive it. But as we grow, we allow more and more things into our consciousness and begin to act on them. Maybe we save one child in our life-time; maybe we only raise our own child without beating him. Maybe we save a child a day. Maybe we play the key role in eliminating forever these 27,000 deaths a day. We're all at different levels of making peace with ourselves concerning our participation on the planet. And that level changes as we go along. Only we can say what peace is for us ourselves. Again this is the greatness of being human: We get to decide our level of creation/participation in the universe.

5. Joy

I am not sure what joy is. When I think about how I described peace, I see joy pretty much as the same thing. But joy is more intense, profound, like seeing something exquisitely beautiful, or rejoicing in your children (This is usually best done while they're sleeping), or having a strong sense of your own being. Maybe it is what Maslow meant by "peak experiences." I apologize for this being such a short section, but I am a novice in this area.

6. Fulfilled expectations

Fulfilled expectations is an over-riding concept and governor of happiness. Simply stated, it means that when you expect something and you get it, you are happy. When you don't get it, you are unhappy. There are, then, two roads to happiness: Get what you want, or don't want anything! The West seems to focus on the first way: Set goals and achieve them (and then, set some more). The East seems to focus more on: He who wants nothing will never be disappointed. Mystics, contemplatives, ascetics, hermits seem to achieve happiness in this way. I once tried to be contemplative, for a year at any rate, but it now seems like a sterile way of life. However, each person is the final arbiter of his own happiness.

Perhaps a third, wiser road to happiness combines both ways of looking at expectations: How about if we had expectations, rejoiced when they were fulfilled, and rejoiced when they weren't fulfilled? We rejoice in living in reality, which means living in and accepting "now," the present, whether our expectations were fulfilled or not. Happiness is shaping reality to fit our expectations and then shaping our expectations to meet reality. This is variation of the Serenity prayer, or the prayer which I gave earlier: "Oh lord, let whatever happens happen." But I am encroaching on the next chapter on **Happiness – How To Find It**.

Summary

We use several words to describe what happiness is: physical well-being, fun and pleasure, security, peace, joy, fulfilled expectations. Most happiness seems to devolve around the last: we are happy when our expectations are fulfilled. Yet, we can also create happiness by accepting what's so when our expectations aren't fulfilled.

Chapter 27:

HAPPINESS–HOW TO FIND IT

How do you find happiness?

From what I said at the end of the last chapter, we don't find happiness; we create it. People who are unhappy may say something like: "That's easy for you to say. You are probably a rich evangelist who has everything you need. What about poor people; how do they create happiness?" Poor people can create happiness the same way rich people do: They change their attitude. They make up their mind to be happy by getting what they want or wanting what they get.

Yet, happiness is not just a question of making up your mind. What if you are really unhappy, and you say, "Oh, I'm happy!" That's lying, isn't it? Yes and no. On the one hand, if you are in pain or you don't feel peaceful or secure, then you don't feel happy. On the other hand there is something you can do in every circumstance to become happy, and that is up to you. Here is the "Rule of Happiness" which will enable you to confront all unhappiness.

The Rule of Happiness: Change it or choose it.

The Rule of Happiness is: Change it or choose it. To become happy in life, all we need to do is consciously make

171

a choice in any given situation: Change the situation or choose the situation. I am in charge of every circumstance in my life. Although I may not have created the circumstance, I have the option to change it. If I can't change it or choose not to, I have the option of choosing it, of accepting things the way they are. It is never the circumstances in life which determine happiness; it is how I react to them. These are the only two valid choices regarding any circumstance. The other choices are "invalid" choices. (Not a bad play on words, eh?) We make invalids of ourselves when we make in-valid choices; namely, we become the victim of our circumstances. There are people who really are invalids, people with wretched circumstances in life. Am I suggesting that these people "choose" their circumstances? Of course I am; or, see if they can change them. Stop whining. We're all going to die anyhow!

But let's not worry about other people. Take a look at yourself. If something is negative in your life, change it or choose it. Don't whine about it, don't rail at it, don't endure it. Say: "This is the way things are. This is what's on my plate. I choose to have things be the way they are." Don't be a victim in life, or, in the that felicitous phrasing of George Bernard Shaw, don't be " . . . a feverish selfish little clod of ailments and grievances complaining that the world will not devote itself to making you happy." The distinction between pain and suffering is that pain is the fact, the circumstance, and suffering is the interpretation we make of it. Pain is what happens – what you experience, the physical feeling of hurt. We can react to it in two ways: change it or choose it. If you can do anything to relieve the pain, go for it, do it, change it. If you can't change it you still have two options: One is to suffer: "Oh my god, this is terrible, why did this happen to me, this always happens to me, I hate this, I'm really mad at everybody, at the universe, etc." All of this is the interpretation we add to the experience of pain. The other way to react is to adopt the attitude: this is the way it is. Have the pain without creating a lot of drama around it. That is what choosing it means. You would rather not have it, but it is here. If it is unchangeable, you say, "Let's move on."

Sometimes "changing it" only involves changing your mind, that is, giving up expectations. How long do you stay mad at the rain? Perhaps this is the key to happiness. How fast are you able to give up your pictures of what things should be, or what you wanted them to be, and accept how they really are? Or, how fast are you at creating plan B when plan A is not producing the results you want? This kind of thinking takes responsibility for our lives. It means taking on our sacred role of creator.

If you are finding this line of thinking difficult to accept, especially from the viewpoint that there are people who do have harsh lives, people who actually are victimized, I want to quote three people whom I respect. The first, Victor Frankl, was a psychologist who was is a concentration camp for a long period of time. In *Man's Search for Meaning* he shares what he experienced and learned – that even though you may be in victimizing circumstances, you have a choice about whether you will take on the role of victim or not. Even in those terrible circumstances that would seem to justify giving up, some people did not act as if they were victims. He says: "They may be few in number, but they offer sufficient proof that everything can be taken from a man but one thing: The last of human freedoms – to choose one's attitude in any given set of circumstances, to choose one's own way."

The second person is Job – the man from the *Bible* who had a great wife, family, house, herds, etc. Then, it was all taken away from him, and he's sitting on a dunghill. Here's what he says: "The Lord gives and the lord takes away; blessed be the name of the Lord." Sometimes we find it difficult to adopt this attitude. Here's how I like to look at it. First of all, nobody has a <u>right</u> to the goods of the earth; they are all gifts. Sunshine and peaches and oil and cotton and the love of others are all gifts. Nobody has a right to life; it is a gift. Our very presence here is a gift. So, to focus on what we do not have is to presume we have a right to what we do have. We have the right to nothing. It is all a gift to which gratefulness is the appropriate response. When circumstances go against us, we need to focus on what we have, not the loss of what we no longer have. One second of existence is a gift; two seconds is better.

The third quote is a prayer from the theologian, Reinhold Neibuhr. You are probably familiar with the prayer, but I bet you didn't know that Neibuhr was the source. It is commonly called the "serenity prayer." It goes something like this:

"Lord, grant me the serenity to accept the things I can't change, the courage to change the things I can change and the wisdom to know the difference."

The serenity part corresponds to the "choose it" option, and of course the courage part is the "change it" option. Serenity means that you are clear that you cannot or will not change the situation, and you actually choose it. That is, you don't resent it, or endure it, or resist it, or pretend that it's okay. You have it be okay. that things are exactly as they are. On the other hand, why does it take courage to change something? Usually because there is some risk or trade-off involved. That is why change is not easy. Risk means it may not work out positively for us. Or, to take option A means that I have to give up option B. Courage means you are willing to make the trade-off or to take a risk, to move forward in the face of uncertainty.

How does one get to wisdom, though? In two ways: First, wisdom often boils down to courage in a lot of cases. How can you know for sure whether you can change a situation or not? Try to change it. Then you will know whether it is changeable or not! The second way to get wisdom is to communicate, either with yourself or by speaking to someone else. We often can figure things out ourselves by just writing or speaking about them .

I see three theories behind the "Rule of Happiness":

- First, happiness is relative. A man without socks can be grateful he has shoes. A man with a million dollars can be ungrateful that he doesn't have two million. In either case they can move forward or stay where they are. They both have the possibility to move forward, to have goals and then to be happy if they reach their goals, or, as Job, to be happy if they don't reach them.

Happiness is also relative if we compare ourselves to others. As *Desiderata* says, don't compare yourself to others. You will find one who is better off than you and become envious, or find one who is worse off and become proud.

• Secondly, happiness comes from both end result and process. Getting <u>there</u> counts, and <u>getting</u> there counts. Happiness comes from balancing a goal orientation and a process orientation. Some goal-oriented people are bent on pursuing one goal after another after another. They are in a mad rush to the grave. When they reach it, they say: "I've finally gotten here!" They forgot to smell the roses along the way! They forgot that the <u>getting</u> there, the process, counts too! In this time-bound world most of us need to set goals so that we have something we're moving toward. We can put up with hardships during the process of getting there because we're happy to achieve the goal or result. Yet, if we don't pull back and look at the process periodically – "Yes, I am moving toward my goal, but is it worth it?" – we may be missing out on life.

On the other hand some people are bent on enjoying only the process of life, the here and now. Living in the moment is great, but living for the moment may not be. We have to pay attention to the future because we may consume all of our resources now and have nothing in the future.

Happiness comes from balance, from gracefully shifting our focus between end result and process.

• Thirdly, happiness is totally self-initiated, since there are no "have to's" in life. You don't <u>have</u> to change anything, and you don't <u>have</u> to choose anything. We are free to choose whatever will make us happy. Our role is to be co-creators of the universe. Part of our job is to receive the gifts of the universe in gratitude; part is to use the gifts to further the progress of the universe. There are no rules as to where and how far we can go. We get to make them up ourselves.

To summarize, we are here to share this incredible opportunity to maximize life – our own life, the life of the planet, and the life of the universe. Every circumstance in life is an opportunity to forward life, whether or not we initially view it as such. It is irresponsible to whine in the face of any opportunity. What is responsible is to accept the opportunity, either by using it, changing it, or choosing it. Here is a variation of the "Rule of Happiness": Have what you choose, or choose what you have. A victim is someone who doesn't take responsibility for life. When I am acting the victim, either I don't have what I choose, i.e., I don't go out after what I want, take the next step in moving forward, or I don't choose what I have. I choose instead to complain and moan and grumble and whine about it, instead of making the best of it. When I am acting as co-creator, everything truly is an opportunity.

One other thought on finding happiness; Order my book, *Don't Go to Work Unless It's Fun: State-of-the-Heart Time Management!*

In conclusion, I think Abraham Lincoln said the wisest thing about happiness: "A man is about as happy as he makes up his mind to be."

Summary

To be happy, follow The Rule of Happiness: Change it or choose it. That is, if you are not happy change your situation – do something to have things become the way you want them to be. Or, choose it – have it be okay that things are exactly the way they are. Part of "choosing it" means to give up your expectations when you see they won't be met. The three reasons this rule works are:

- Happiness is relative. We can always make our selves unhappy by comparing ourselves to others, or by comparing what we got with what we wanted.

- Happiness comes from both end result – having goals and working toward them – and process – enjoying the journey here and now. More precisely, happiness comes from balancing the two, shifting focus between them when appropriate.

- Happiness comes from taking responsibility for being a co-creator of the universe. This means two things: being grateful for the gifts we have, using them to create a better universe, and not worrying about the things we don't have. Or, go out and get the gifts you want.

Lincoln had the best thing to say about happiness: "A man is about as happy as he makes up his mind to be." Happiness, similar to the meaning of life, is a decision we make.

Section 5:

MISCELLANEOUS STUFF

Chapter 28:

REINTERPRETING CHRISTIAN DOGMAS

Since I was brought up in what is called the Christian tradition, I want to re-visit some fundamental Christian beliefs. I say "what is called the Christian tradition" because there is no such thing "as the Christian tradition." Look at not only all the divisions in Christianity, but the differences in belief of individual Christians. Most Christian dogmas, as other myths, are valid inasmuch as they point to some truth. The trick is to not get caught up in the myth or metaphor, but to discover the underlying truth. When we take the metaphor literally, and it conflicts with fact or data, we get in trouble by having to choose between metaphor and data. I thought it would be interesting to revisit some doctrines from the viewpoint of what could possibly be the underlying truth in some Christian doctrines now that I have given up virtually all of the stories or myths in which the truth is enshrouded. My approach to doing this is to simply ask "How could they have come up with this belief?"

Did Jesus rise from the dead?

Jesus' literal resurrection from the dead, of course, seems

to be the pivotal belief of Christianity. My opinion is that it is highly unlikely that he did. The problem is that either you have a body or you don't. If he has a body, where is it? Where did he go – Uranus? Alpha Centauri? If he went to "heaven" that means that heaven would have to be a physical place. But from my discussion of after-life and physicality, this is contradictory. Physical can't be eternal. Yet, isn't it possible that his body is <u>somewhere</u>, outside of our finite comprehension? Yes, it is possible, but then my principle kicks in: If you can't know something, it doesn't make any difference. Perhaps his followers saw something non-physical? But how can you see something non-physical? That again is contradictory. When someone sees something that is not physically there, we say they are hallucinating.

The early Christians could have been hallucinating, or they may have just made up this story of Jesus rising from the dead. Why would they do that? We can get an insight from looking at the Elvis Presley phenomenon. People continue to claim he is still alive. If you think somebody was very important, that is how you give him stature. Early Christians wanted to point out that this man was a unique guy and had some very special things to say which were important to listen to. So, if we have him rise from the dead, that would be unique! People will pay attention. What the heck, why not go a step further and make him god?

The "Trail of Doctrines"

The last question above is not gratuitous: If Jesus rose from the dead, why not make him a god? Or, if he is a god, why not have him rise from the dead? If you make up one story, then other stories follow from it. This gives an insight into what I call the "trail of doctrines." If you start from one premise, then a lot of other things don't make sense. So, you have to make up new stories to justify the last premise or story. I map out this trail as I see it. I didn't research the order in which doctrines appeared and have absolutely no interest in doing so (if it can even be done). I am just looking at it rationally and trying to piece together, "How did they come up with <u>this</u> one?" These are the answers I come up with.

For example, if Jesus rose from the dead, the logical question is, "Where is he?" So, the early writers and church invented the Ascension. It was a cover-up. (The Assumption came along later – why leave his mom out?) Then we have the really big one: "Hey, if he rose from the dead, he must be eternal, he must be god."

Was Jesus god?

Was Jesus really god? The answer is yes and no. Yes, in exactly the same sense that any of us is "god" – we participate in the universe and have a unique role in creating the universe to be what it is/is becoming. No, in the sense that it would be unseemly to have a god nailed to a cross and to suffer the other slings and arrows of outrageous fortune that flesh is heir to (remember, all this presumes a belief in an outie god to begin with.). That's why the theologians had to invent the Holy Trinity. Once you make Jesus god, it requires a lot of fancy footwork (or footnotes). Otherwise people would say, "You mean the guy who made this whole show and keeps it going was just killed by some minor stage hands? No way."

Trinity

The next step in the trail of doctrines, then, is the invention of the "Trinity." (I remember telling an intelligent friend once that theologians were speculating on a Quaternity. Instead of laughing, he interestedly asked me, "What do they say?") Trinity answers the question: How can Jesus be god and not god at the same time? The rationale is this: You need to distinguish him from an outie creator of the universe, or "father." Let's call Jesus the "son." Okay, now we can kill the son part. That would be a little more palatable. Up here in the sky you have the father, whom nobody can mess with. Then, when the son does something that can not be associated with god, you say: "Oh, that is his humanity part." Where does the holy spirit come in? Through the rafters on Pentecost! I guess truly amazing things happened to the early Christians – they received extraordinary insights, feelings, strength, vision, sense of community, purpose. So much so, that they thought: I'm in-"spired;" I'm "breathed into." This is so good it must be a holy breath, a "holy spirit." Oh, this is how god/Jesus is going to be with us from now on, through this gift of the holy spirit.

Holy Spirit

The trail brings us to the holy spirit as a way of explaining godly things happening to us and within us. This is how god/Jesus (i.e., Father/Son) is still with us. Yet, on a rational level, we can also consider the things that they experienced as similar to what we all experience in varying degrees during every day life, things naturally available to everybody. We can always say that the "spirit" is with us – thoughts, and insights, and feelings, and heartbeats are all a stream of on-going gifts. Every breath – "spiritus" – is a gift. When I take a look at all this stuff I'm writing, it is all a gift given to me. I am making it up, just like everybody else who writes about god. It's what we theologians mean by "inspiration." Where does it come from? We don't know. So, we can say that <u>everything</u> is a special gift. We don't need some special guy to pop down and deliver it just because it seems like an extra special gift today.

All of this discussion is based on the highly implausible theory of an outie god, a someone distinct and separate from the universe, who created it. Even though this is implausible to me, there may still be some value in using the "trinity as a metaphor. We can still keep these underlying realities:

1. Father means: the universe, including me, is, and it is good. Maybe the universe came to be, or maybe it just is, but I definitely came to be and am the recipient of infinite gifts that make my life possible. I have been "fathered."

2. Son means: Jesus was a great person, who profoundly received and shared the gifts of the world. We too have that same special capacity to receive, share and create.

3. Holy Spirit means: Everything that exists, all life, is a gift. At every moment we share in the forward thrust, or intelligent unified energy of the universe.

Virgin birth

The virgin birth is another Catholic doctrine that can be understood if you follow the trail of doctrines and accept the premise that Jesus was god. If god was his father, how could he have had a human father, Joseph? "Well, Joseph wasn't his <u>real</u> father; his real father is god. Hey, here's a good job for the Holy Spirit. We'll let him impregnate Mary." I can imagine Joseph talking to Mary when she announces that she's pregnant: "Wait a minute. Let's get this straight. You're kneeling there and this big bird flies in and then what happens?"

One unfortunate turn that the trail of doctrines had, I mentioned in the sex chapter. If Mary was a virgin, virginity must be good. If virginity is good, sex must be bad. Of course, I am just surmising all of this, but you have to wonder why Christians and especially Catholics are so down on sex.

Paradise/Heaven

Further along on the Trail of Doctrines: If Jesus can live forever, so can we! I spoke of the implausibility of this in the chapter on **Afterlife**. Christians think of Paradise as both the original "blessed" state and also where we go after we die. My reinterpretation of the garden of Eden or paradise is that it was neither at the beginning nor at the end in some other place. It is something that we are partially in right now, and something we are partially moving toward but on earth. We are half-way there from barbarity. The global glass is half empty or half full, depending on how you look at it. For example, we barbarously allow 27,000 people (at this edit) to die every day who don't need to. On the other hand, about half the world's countries have ended hunger as a basic issue. The earth and life is a great place to be. This is as good as it gets – and as bad as it gets. We are in heaven and hell right now. So, we are both in paradise, or heaven, and moving toward it at the same time.

The best we can do is live now in the paradise that exists at this time. You and I won't be here when paradise is achieved on earth, but there will come a day when all children live, when all have a chance to make their contribution, when the environment is cared for, when money is a tool rather than a master. Yet even then, higher goals will be sought. If something better does come along – heaven, paradise, a messiah, a redeemer – I will take it, but I am not waiting. Given my record in the stock market, it will come the day after I sell.

Original Sin

I am not sure where original sin comes in the trail of doctrines. Perhaps people wondered why this isn't the ultimate paradise here and now. Life is hard often; maybe it is our fault. So if we say we have original sin, then something is wrong with us and we don't deserve paradise. Yet, one can ask, "Did Jesus die to atone for our sins or was original sin invented to explain why he died?"

In any case, original sin is neither sin nor original. Sin implies we did something and therefore we are something bad. However, in opposition to this thought, two things: First, we didn't do anything bad. We just happen to be here, arriving as babies. Secondly, we are not anything bad. We are good. As I quoted earlier, "God don't make no junk." As individuals and as a race, we continue to grow out of our immaturity into the fullness of being. Read my chapter on **Sin**. Also read Matthew Fox's *Original Blessing*. Likewise with the "original" part, there is nothing different between the first man (I forgot his name) and us. Any "differences" are just a matter of degree. All of humankind and each of us individually is on a path of growth – with many setbacks. So the way that the first man was, that we are and the last man will be is all the same – with all the changes of evolution thrown in, of course. Original sin was invented to explain our barbarous side, our undeveloped side, our whining side.

Redemption

It follows that if something is wrong with us, if we are

guilty of original sin, we need redemption. We need someone to appease the irate master, to pay back something for
our being bad. If, on the other hand, the universe is unfolding itself as it should, we don't need it. Redemption
was invented by whiners who did not like the way things
were. So they said something was wrong with this life,
which justified waiting for something better to come along.
Let me preach to you here: Look at the full half of the glass
and work for kindness in your life, which really means
work for fairness, justice. This is all there is to do anyhow.
After that is achieved, we can all work at creating better
games to play, better, even, than golf or handball. This is
my interpretation of "redeeming the world."

Miracles

What about miracles? Do miracles happen? Yes and no.
The miracle of existence itself in all its glory – yes. One of
the privileges of aging is to be able to see more often what
a splendid, improbable miracle the existence of me, of us
all, of the universe is. Besides this, one might call the de-
lightful serendipities that happen in life miracles. To push
it further, people may have hallucinations and powerful
wishful thinking that cause them to interpret what happens as a miracle. Many things can be called miracles. But,
no, miracles do not happen if you mean that it is possible
to bend or contradict the harmonious and consistent ways
in which the universe operates.

Grace

One last thing: What is grace? It is an unnecessary middle
man. I am thinking of the line in the hymn *Amazing Grace*
— "'Twas grace that taught my heart to fear, and grace
that fear relieved." If grace hadn't come around in the first
place to teach us to fear, it would have saved itself and
everybody a lot of trouble from having to come around a
second time to relieve it! I am just playing a little here, but
the point is that we don't need any special intervention in
history for grace to be brought to us. It is already here. It
has been here since the big bang. I again go back to the

etymology of the word: gratia or gratis, "freely given." Everything in the universe is grace. We have already been "saved," received grace, just by being here!

Summary

Most Christian doctrines, as other myths, are valid inasmuch as they point to some underlying truth. The trick is to not get caught up in the myth or metaphor, but to discover the underlying truth. When we take the metaphor literally, and it conflicts with other truths, we get into trouble. We are forced to choose between a metaphor and a fact rather than accepting all the truths that underlie the metaphors.

Because early Christians believed one story, they were then forced to make up other stories for the sake of consistency. They created a "trail of doctrines." I have no interest in researching which doctrines historically came first, but I have shared some of my speculations in this chapter. Of course, I have reinterpreted these doctrines in a way that makes sense to me.

The basic truths underlying the fundamental doctrine in Christianity, the trinity, are:

1. Father means: the universe, including me, is, and it is good. Maybe the universe came to be, or maybe it just is, but I definitely came to be and am the recipient of infinite gifts that make my life possible. I have been "fathered."

2. Son means: Jesus was a great person, who profoundly received and shared the gifts of the universe. We too have that same special capacity to receive and give.

3. Holy Spirit means: At every moment we share in the forward thrust, or intelligent unified energy of the universe. All life is a gift that keeps on giving.

Chapter 29:

MINOR CATHOLIC DOCTRINE JOKES

I attempted to write the original version of this book in a humorous vein. The effectiveness of that effort is a moot point. However, in this rewrite, I decided to include at least one chapter for the sake of humor and irreverence. Some of these jokes are ancient. Here goes:

Q: What does the Italian atheist believe?
A: There is no god, and Mary is his mother.

Q: Why did the Holy Spirit appear on Pentecost?
A: Because it was a holy day of obligation and he knew all the Christians would be there.

Q: Why did he appear in tongues of fire?
A: The tongue is the only part of the body that generates saliva; hence it could constantly protect itself from the flame.

Q: Why do Catholics get confused about Mary being god?
A: Because she was a good dresser and early Christians said, "Doesn't she look divine!"

Q: What did Aaron say to Moses when Moses came down the mountain and told him the terms of the covenant? (In case your missed this one earlier!)

A: "Wait a minute, let me get this straight. The Arabs get the land with all the oil under it, and we get to cut off the tips of our penises?"

Q: Why did god choose circumcision as the sign of the covenant?
A: He wanted to see if the Hebrews could take a joke. (It is similar to when he told Abraham to kill Isaac.) Unfortunately, when all the Hebrews took him seriously, he didn't have the heart to tell them he was just kidding.

Q: Why did the Catholic Church repeal the Feast of the Circumcision as a holy day of obligation?
A: I am not going to touch this one.

Q: How is it that god created light on the first day but didn't create the sun and stars until the fourth day?
A: God gets very annoyed at embarrassing questions. This is one of them, so shut the hell up.

Q: Speaking of which, is there really a hell?
A: Yes, for people who ask questions like the last one. Also, for people who have children and who are at their wits end to try to think up something to scare the hell out of them, so to speak.

Q: How many angels can dance on the head of a pin?
A: It depends. Are we talking fox-trot, the rumba, line dancing, slam dancing, moshing?

Q: How could Jesus have said, "If thy eye scandalize thee, pluck it out."
A: He didn't mean that literally.

Q: How do interpreters and preachers decide what to take literally and what not to?
A: It is a mystery.

Q: What are the Cardinal virtues?
A: Good hitting, good pitching and bullpen strength. But they lack slugging strength. (This was true back in the

early to mid-90s, when I first wrote this book, according to George Heroux.)

Q: Is money the root of all evil?
A: No, the <u>lack</u> of it is.

Q: What is Extreme Unction?
A: It is that with which the richest preachers speak.

Q: What does "washed in the blood of the lamb" mean?
A: It is a more natural process that is becoming popular since they banned red dye #4.

Q: Why did they canonize St. Gemma?
A: She was the first Italian girl to say "no."

Q: Why do they use the word "canonize"?
A: It fits in with other Church military terminology like "Onward Christian Soldiers," or taking Holy Orders. Perhaps it means that you are now a big shot in the church.

Q: What did god say to Joan of Arc when she got to heaven?
A: "Well done, good and faithful servant."

Q: Why did the blessed virgin appear at Lourdes, Fatima and Guadeloupe?
A: Because these are popular tourist spots for Catholics.

Q: What did she say when she recently appeared at the national Catholic shrine in Washington?
A: I want you to build me a beautiful church in this place.

Q: Why does the Pope choose to be called the Vicar of Christ?
A: Because it sounds less stuffy than "Wakefield."

Q: Why were we taught that hell is a place of unspeakable suffering, and that if there were a mountain of iron one mile high and a bird flew past every thousand years and its wing just brushed against the mountain, that by the time the mountain was worn away, hell would just be beginning?

A: That was a gross exaggeration. The bird flew by every <u>hundred</u> years.

Summary

I couldn't leave without sharing some smart-ass remarks and ancient jokes. If strong Christians made a mistake and read this book despite my warning, and you are offended, then it's your own damn fault!

Chapter 30:

SUMMARY OF THE TEN GREAT SELF-EVIDENT TRUTH/BELIEFS

One of the benefits of my giving a summary of the ten great self-evident truth/beliefs is that if you are flipping through this book in the bookstore and you want to get the "meat" out of this book without buying it, here it is! I came up with the number 10 because 10 is a special number having mystical meaning going back into the dim mists of pre-history. More accurately, it is probably not unrelated to the fact that we happen to have 10 fingers, so it was a convenient number to come up with. Also, when you pick a number out of the air, it is amazing how your brain can actually come up with the exact number of ideas to match the number you picked.

Why are these truth/beliefs **great**? They're very freeing, basic ideas to replace religious ideas that were freeing at first but may have become enslaving. It's like the shift from Ptolemy to Copernicus. Hey, did you know that right as I'm writing this book the Pope came out and said, after only 300 years, that Galileo was right after all! I remember my father telling me this story: At the end of his trial Galileo told the churchmen, "What could I have been thinking? Of course the earth doesn't move around the sun!" On the way out of the court house, however, he mumbles, "E pur, si muove – "Still, it moves!" I am also reminded about the pope's visit to South America a few years ago when he told them not to use the birth control pill. All the women turned to each other and said, "There's a pill?" At any rate I consider these truth/beliefs great because they are fundamental beliefs which shift our picture of the universe, and they are a foundation which underlies all beliefs.

Why are they **self-evident**? They seem so to me. If they're not evident to you, cross out the ones you don't like, and put in your own. In fact, make up your own list. If you actually do that, this book will have achieved its purpose. The gift I am giving to you is the opportunity to re-examine and formulate what's so for yourself. These beliefs are what's so for me.

Why do I call them **truth/beliefs**? If I presented them as truths, some people might take them as absolute truth, create a new cult, deify me and send money. None of these is a very good outcome, except the money part. (Credit cards accepted.) But going back to the chapter on **Faith**, truth is fact plus interpretation of fact. Since even fact or data is received through the filter of human perception, the facts themselves are interpretations of what's out there. So it would be presumptuous of me to call them "truths," just as it is presumptuous for anybody to "speak great truths" and not be open to question or challenge. However, if I just called them "beliefs," people might not take them seriously and discount them by saying: "Oh, these are just his beliefs." They are beliefs, but they are the most profound I can come up with.

Without further ado, here are:

THE TEN GREAT SELF-EVIDENT TRUTH/BELIEFS

1. If you can't know or find out something for sure, then it doesn't matter.

2. We create the meaning of life.

3. The universe exists. That's all we can say about god for sure.

4. Laws, moral or natural, are descriptions of what happens.

5. Whether there is an afterlife or not makes no difference. (Refer back to #1.)

6. Don't bring god in to justify belief or action. We hold our beliefs simply because we choose to and for no other reason. We also do "good" or "bad" things out of choice — either the positive choice to do something or the negative choice of not getting help to control compulsive behavior.

7. The best question to ask about any belief is: What difference would it make if I didn't believe this? This question helps get to the value underlying the belief, which is the important thing.

8. We are the magnificent co-creators of the universe. Creation continues now, and we are part of making it happen.

9. There is a natural, fundamental response to all things in the universe. The name we give to that response in "love."

10. The universe demands a respect for what's so, whether we like it or not. Learn to dance with the universe. The universe leads.

Summary

Go back and re-read these ten things. How fundamental can I get!

Section 6:

A CHURCH FOR THE MILLENNIUM

Chapter 31:

OVERVIEW FOR A NEW CHURCH

As I mentioned earlier, we need some kind of "structure of fulfillment" for humanity to become all that we were meant to be, or, more accurately, all that we mean ourselves to be. For want of a more powerful term, let's call it a church. I use the word "church" advisedly. The deepest strivings and understanding of mankind have always been associated with god, religion, and – using my western, American and personal bias – a church. For me the word symbolizes a community of people who focus on the meaning of life – to understand it and to fulfill it. For humanity to come to be fully, we need to create a community of people committed to do that. We need a new church! Don't say, "Oh god, not another church." When you read about this concept of a church, you will realize that most current churches would consider it an anti-church.

The **purpose** of such a church would be, very simply, to create a world that works for everyone. That implies a structure that allows the growth of both the individual and the community of man. It facilitates each individual in pursuing their own personal and spiritual growth in an optimum way, and it allows us together to heal and fulfill the planet and perhaps even the universe. It is no less than that sacred purpose which we need to pursue.

Such a church needs a theological foundation, a bedrock on which to stand. That is the first thing I will discuss. Then we will look at the two great needs in the world, i.e., a world that works for me and a world that works for everyone else. I use the word "integration" to encompass these two needs. We need to be on the on-going path of integrating our own individual lives into greater harmony, and we need to integrate the world so that no one is left out. We are at a crossroads of history where the decisions we make about poverty, population and environment will profoundly affect the kind of world there is in the future. To fulfill its mission, such a church will provide the best means to pursue personal internal integrity and external global integrity.

However, there two great lacks in the world which prevent us from fulfilling those needs. Traditional churches, for the most part, don't function in a way that best fulfills these two needs, and, secondly, other institutions in the world aren't designed to do be able to fulfill them. Current churches do not support the growth of their members in the most effective way, and they don't seem to work toward integrating the world. In fact, most of them, in practice, are exclusionary and actually foster divisiveness in the world. Current secular institutions are not doing any better. Most other institutions, by definition, pursue limited, not universal, goals. What is called for is a turbo-charged effort to "save the world," literally. Yet governments, businesses, etc. are taking a horse and buggy approach, if any at all, to do so.

What does a church that seriously tackles these issues look like? For individuals it provides an ongoing forum of support to explore and pursue spiritual and personal growth – a world that works for me. For mankind it marshals human energy to resolve critical social issues and create a

197

global community – a world that works for everyone. A structure is called for where people can speak honestly with each other, listen to everybody's views, acknowledge the needs of all and work towards consensus. There is no need for a pope, imam, rabbi, bishop, priest, minister, etc. There are infinitely more ideas in the body of humanity than in any individual. We need a safe space where people can express their thinking and explore where they are going and where they think the world should be going. We need a "bottom-up" church rather than a "top-down" one.

The next chapters describe some of the details for what I have just outlined.

Summary

We need a new church whose purpose is to create a world that works for everyone.

Chapter 32:

THEOLOGICAL FOUNDATION: BEDROCK

A church needs a foundation, a theological bedrock to stand on. We want to answer the questions: What can I really count on? What is absolutely true? What will give me the surest footing in life, a fundamental ground to stand on? Since I have already answered these questions, let me give a brief summary of the theology that I presented earlier: First, every individual is sacred. Secondly, all beliefs are relative. These two beliefs are what constitute the theological bedrock for such a church to stand on. That's it, nothing more. And if all beliefs are relative, you don't even have to believe these to be part of the church!

You pause, gentle reader. Looking at the paucity of dogma that I have come up with, you may not be very pleased. "Are you trying to be ironic?" you say. "All that your dogma says is that there is no dogma; we make it all up ourselves! How does that give anyone surety? What kind of a foundation is that to stand on?" To answer that on a personal level, having traveled down the other road of uncritically buying into a system of dogmatic belief, I find this road to be a much more refreshing, empowering and surer breath of life for me.

199

Since, however, I presume you are concerned about finding the road for yourself, I have laid out my personal thinking as well as I could for you to have something to bump up against to formulate your own thinking.

Let me briefly explore the theology represented by these two beliefs. The first belief is that everything, everybody, each one of us is sacred. We all are, all exist, and by virtue of that we all are sacred, holy, divine. This theory may well be a modern description of the old concept, pantheism. We are all part of the forward thrust or intelligent unified energy of the universe. Our being gives us, de facto, our sacredness. This belief in the sacredness of every individual gives rise to creating a world that reverences and works for everyone.

The second belief – that all beliefs are relative – is the foundation of a truly universal church. "Relative" means that beliefs are our own inventions. They are stories we invent about data or facts, which serve us and create meaning. A belief is a construct which helps us to understand the universe, and which gives value to our life. Evidence can be found to support diametrically opposed beliefs. As I said earlier, one church is as good as another, if it provides value. But that's not how churches usually think of themselves. Many defensively say, "We're the best! We're right (and you're not)!" Yet true churches are inclusive, not exclusive. Given that requirement, the only true church is one which includes all of humanity, and therefore all belief systems. The dogma that all beliefs are relative (including this one) is the only foundation for any truly universal church. Any more dogma added to that begins to destroy universality. Beyond (and including) these two principles, everything is relative.

Summary

On these two theological bedrock principles everything stands: First, every individual is sacred. Secondly, all beliefs are relative.

Chapter 33:

TWO GREAT NEEDS

What is needed in the world today, which most current churches and institutions don't seem to address or provide directly? The words "integration" or "integrity" seem to that best answer that question. The Oxford English Dictionary defines integration as: "the making up of a whole by adding together separate parts; the harmonious combination of the different elements in a personality." Harmonious wholeness is missing on two levels, individual and global. A workable church provides integration or integrity on both of these levels. On the level of the individual it provides a world that works for me, that enables me to achieve integrity in my own life. On a global level is provides a vehicle for a world that works for everyone, that affords everyone the opportunity not only to live, but to live a full, rich life. Let's explore these two need more fully.

1. Internal Integration: A world that works for me

Internal integration means that individuals becomes integrated within themselves, that they have the opportunity and support to fulfill themselves physically, mentally, emotionally, and spiritually. A church should provide a place for people to keep growing harmoniously. Modern society militates against this. If you want your body taken care of, you go to a doctor. For your emotions, you go to a psychologist. For your mind, you go to school. For your spirit, theoretically, you go to a church. Yet, we all function as a unit, as one, as an integrated person.

In addition, we have a variety of roles in our lives. Sometimes I am a father, sometimes a spouse, a businessman, a citizen, a friend, and so on. We have so many roles that it is often difficult to sense: who is the real me? We need integrity, the harmonious wholeness of all our parts and roles working together, and reaching their full potential.

Let's take a look at a few attitudes and conditions which cause our lives not to work, because they militate against personal integrity.

1. Scarcity: Not enough time, money, etc.

In the workshops I have been teaching for many years I have been helping people have enough time, enough money, abundance in all parts of their lives. I see many unhappy people: "Why is it that I gross a quarter of a million dollars and can't make ends meet? Why do I bill out my time at $185 an hour and still worry financially? Why do I work 50 or 60 hours a week? Why does it seem that I can't balance my personal and work life?" Of course, much of the resolution to those issues comes about by reengineering our attitudes, our interpretations of reality. I see that if people had a support group to regularly talk to about themselves, and to explore what it would take to get out of their misery, they could go very far in alleviating their pain and in creating abundance. You might call it a "Peace of Mind" group.

2. Victimhood

Many people feel that their life is not within their control. We feel victimized by our circumstances rather than taking responsibility for our lives and using our power to change them. This applies to all of us in varying degrees. We blame our unhappiness on our conditions, rather than on ourselves. Or more accurately, we don't take responsibility to stop thinking in terms of blame of others or ourselves, and to get on with discovering and fulfilling our fundamental needs. It does not take rocket science to do this. Through self-exploration and sharing on a regular basis, we can begin to shape our lives.

3. Permanent white water; people always in transition

I was going to start by saying, "In the olds days, life was stable and relatively unchanging." However, that probably is not true. What may be true is that things changed at a less rapid pace before the technological age, but they still changed. However, I recently heard a phrase that seems to describe our present times: "the speed of life." The speed of life approaches the speed of light. Has technology simplified your life? I doubt it. Technology just ups the stakes of what we demand of ourselves and others. In addition, people are always transitioning in their lives. I forget what the seven stages of life are or what stages Gail Sheehy identifies in *Passages*, but it is clear that no matter what our age, each of us can say that we are changing and society around us is changing more rapidly than when we were younger. We seem to get caught up in the swirl of things, and it is very difficult to create times for ourselves to locate our center.

4. Busy-ness — The tyranny of the urgent

I suppose being busy is just another way of saying all of the above. Earlier I gave the quote: "Experience without reflection is not educative; it's just one damn thing after the other." I also love the enigmatic saying of Pascal: "I have discovered that all human evil comes from this: a man's being unable to sit still in a room." Isn't it also interesting that the word "business" derives from "busy-ness." Truly, it is generally business – the job of earning a living – that creates most of our busy-ness.

A personal experience about the tyranny of the urgent comes from having my son, Jamie, home from school one day (circa 4th grade). Jamie is very dedicated and conscientious. He won't go to bed unless his homework is finished. He'll spend three hours doing his homework, stay up until 11:00, and get up at 6:30 if he didn't finish it. I think he's wearing himself out. This is not okay with me. His whole day should not be spent in school, in homework, and in busyness. That's how we in our culture spend our days, in work and busyness. Something is radically wrong with our culture if we live that way, if we train our children that way. Why? 90% of Americans are in the top 17% of the world's income group and yet nobody makes enough money. We endlessly accumulate, endlessly are busy, and yet very few of us make the time to be, to create peace of mind. Our culture militates against it. So we have to virtually rip ourselves away from the busyness, to make the time to get a clearer picture of who we are and to shape ourselves and start to reshape our culture.

What we desperately need is the chance to tear ourselves away from these conditions, to do some self-examination, self-reflection, to establish the "tyranny of the important." We also need the opportunity to share our concerns, beliefs, dreams with others. To me, deepening my spirituality means: to become happier and happier with myself, to come to be my truer and truer self, to have a body I like and which serves me, to be at peace, to resolve what seems to stop me from moving forward, to formulate dreams and visions, to pursue those dreams. We need a vehicle for people to regularly look at the questions: "Am I moving forward? What's holding me back? In what way would I like to continue to move forward, to continue to grow?" If the moving forward is simply on a physical level, then that's what needs to be attended to. If it's on an emotional level, that's what needs to be attended to. To develop our spirituality does not mean to develop another "piece" of ourselves; it means to create harmony with all the pieces of ourselves, and thus harmony with the rest of creation. We need integration.

For a church to provide spiritual growth, it must foster the growth of the entire, integrated person. The path of internal integration is long, in fact, life-long. We need a life-long and efficient vehicle to do this. In addition, the sooner we achieve basic internal integration (See the chapter **Growing Up**), the faster we are able to start looking outside of ourselves to the world around us. That brings us to the next great need in the world.

2. External Integration: A world that works for everyone

Besides being responsible for creating a world that works for ourselves, we also need to create a world that works for everyone else. This is not a moral but a natural imperative. Just as your hands can't say, "I don't care about what happens to my legs," each individual needs to realize the interconnectedness of all people, all creation. This is what I mean by "external integration."

The world does not currently work for everyone. Some of the more serious issues we face are:

- The gap between the rich and the poor is growing, and the numbers of the poor are growing. Three billion people live on less than 2 dollars a day.
- Almost one billion are chronically malnourished.
- The need to level off population growth grows more critical every day.
- The environmental degradation created by the industrialized countries, and to a minor degree the third world, is making more and more untenable demands on the planet.
- The wars that pepper our planet, which have their source in the issues above.

These are not separate but integrated issues: Population continues to grow at an unsustainable rate, precisely because the poor don't have the security of knowing their children will survive. The poor are poor because the rich (virtually anyone reading this book) squander a disproportionate share of the world's resources, polluting it while doing so.

When I ask people to come and look at what RESULTS is doing (the group of people I work with to end hunger and extreme poverty), most are too busy. We are tied up with our own lives and needs, and we never, or barely, look at the larger world and our responsibility for it. I am not blaming people for this. It is extremely difficult to rise above the forces of our culture and our old belief systems, to become personally "together" enough, integrated enough to turn our eye outward. A church should enable people to get their own lives together very quickly, so that we have the energy to focus on the world around us. Of course, one good way to get our life together is precisely to stop worrying about it and to start contributing to others around us. In addition, one never has their life totally together anyhow, because we live in relation to everything and everybody else. My personal togetherness, integration, depends on the togetherness of the planet. What else is there to do anyhow but to serve your family, your community, the whole world? This is the thrill and joy of creativity – creating a world that works for everyone.

Solving "The PPE Problem"

Let's take a deeper look at interrelated global issues I mentioned above. Perhaps the largest integration issue is to stop looking at problems in isolation from each other and start to recognize that there is one global problem - as UNICEF calls it, the PPE problem. That stands for Population, Poverty, Environment. In order to solve the environmental problem, we need to solve the population problem; in order to solve the population problem, we need to solve the poverty problem. Any problem is resolvable if we break it down. What would we need to do to break each category down into, say, three further sub-groups? UNICEF and others are doing a good job at this. For example, the three keys to population control might be to lower child mortality rates, empower third world women, and give basic literacy and numercy to all children. The three keys to preventing environmental degradation might be controlling ozone depletion, controlling the greenhouse effect and developing renewable energy sources. The three solutions to the poverty problem might be to eliminate barriers to basic health for all, to extend credit to the poor, especially women, and to challenge economic globalization and the autonomy of trans-national corporations. To further sub-categorize in turn, the three keys to basic healthcare might be full expansion of the TB DOTS program, oral rehydration therapy, and immunization – to counter the world's three biggest preventable killers. And so on. Yet no one group has the mandate or is willing to give itself the mandate to take it all on – a world that works for everyone.

The church I envision would do just this, work on resolving the PPE problem, as well as other key global issues. It would stop looking at problems in isolation. For example, take the "immigration problem." We can't resolve that until we resolve the child mortality problem in Mexico and third world countries. We can't resolve that until we deal with free trade and third world debt which contribute to poverty, and so on. A true church would identify the interrelationship of all these issues and to do it in a way people can readily grasp. It would create ways that each person could work on pieces of the problem while still understanding its relation to the whole. UNICEF's annual *State of the World's Children Report* would be a perfect document to outline the issues that need to be looked at each year.

Virtually all existing institutions are inadequate to cope with the serious issues threatening the world now. As I write this, the U.S. Congress is pushing to "reduce big government" and rely on volunteerism. Although this may be partially an abrogation of responsibility, perhaps a church can supply cohesion to a massive volunteer movement. The root of the word "voluntary" comes from the Latin word "voluntas" which means "will." The verb is "volo" which means "I wish" or "I will it." So when you look at volunteer activity, the only reason it happens is because somebody wishes or wills it. I do it simply because "I say so." This is why we need a church. Governments are interested only in their domain of governance. Businesses do things to make a profit. Many educational institutions and current churches are businesses as well. In addition, the primary motivation in many churches currently is guilt – the idea that you must, you ought to, you should. In a guilt-free church, the only reason you would belong is because you say so. The only reason you would volunteer is because you say so.

Another aspect of voluntarism is this: When you think that less than 20% of the world's population controls 82% of the world's resources (that's virtually anyone reading this book, folks), you say, "what can be done about this?" One direction of thought might be, "well, we have to force people to give up their money." But that never works. That creates confrontation between people. The more powerful thing to do is to resort to voluntarism and to have people confront themselves about the best use of their money. The real question is, "how do you want to make a difference in your life?" which leads to, "how do you want to make a difference with your money?" When people see the inequity in the world and see the difference their money can make, they voluntarily use their money to make a difference.

There is no institution today, with the exception of UNICEF, that is willing to take on the PPE problem, that has the explicit purpose of creating a world that works for everyone – not to mention a world that works for each individual. Let us take a closer look at some of these institutions and why they are not working in the next two chapters.

Summary

The two great needs in the world today are:
    1. Internal Integration: A world that works for me.
    2. External Integration: A world that works for everyone.
    No institution on earth that I know of has undertaken
    to resolve these needs.

Chapter 34:

THE GREAT FAILURE #1: HOW CURRENT CHURCHES FAIL

Simply put, many current churches don't do the job they are supposed to, or do so at great inefficiency and waste of resources. They do not function optimally to meet the needs expressed in the previous chapter – a world that works for the individual and a world that works for everyone. Not that they don't do any good, but they just aren't adequate to the task at hand. It is not because of lack of good will or effort, but because most are exclusive, not inclusive, by their very nature. They are not structured to create a world that works for individuals and for everyone. Let's take a look.

1. Current churches don't create a world that works for individuals

Despite the value that current churches may offer their members, most do not free people; they bind them into belief systems which, at best, are 20% useful and at worst cause people to kill each other. They often do not provide spiritual and personal fulfillment for several reasons. Among them:

- Because of a faulty understanding of the nature of lief, many churches are entrapped rather than liberated by their beliefs.
- Church structure and services are often top-down rather than bottom-up. What the leaders think and say and want is more important than what the members think and say and want.
- They don't provide a harmonious program for achieving both internal individual spiritual growth and external global healing.

What is needed is a "creed of no creed," or at least a creed of the relativity of creeds. The word "creed" comes from the Latin word "credo" — "I believe." Beliefs must be the servants of people, not vice-versa. People must not be the servants of beliefs. In other words, if a belief is not useful to you, does not serve you, you should give up the belief. Beliefs are relative. However, this kind of thinking is diametrically opposed to what many churches ascribe to. Their position is that theirs is the true belief, and anyone who doesn't follow their beliefs is wrong, or unwashed, or condemned to perdition, or ought to be killed — if we carry it to extremes. They act as if life should serve faith rather than faith serve life.

Yet, what is desperately needed is a church that doesn't have "all the answers." Why? People look for the Savior, the Messiah who does have all the answers, who is all-knowing. Yet, this is a self-contradictory impossibility. (Look at the chapters on **The Future and the Present** and **God**.) So many of us are looking for this because we are afraid to take responsibility for our own lives. A knight on a white horse to rescue us is appealing, even a Hitler if need be. Yet, we know that no man can know all. Perhaps that is why they say, "If you see the Buddha on the road, kill him." I have no idea what that phrase means to others, but to me this interpretation fits: If you meet someone who has all the answers, someone to whom you can pledge your life and judgment, kill him! Or, to be less extreme, run away as fast as you can. No one has all the answers. Everyone has some answers. Or, better phrased, everyone has a unique point of view. Since it is a point of view, it can never be absolute; but since it is unique, it has something to offer the whole of humanity.

What is needed in a church is not one person's creed, or one fixed dogma, but a forum for sharing all beliefs, all points of view, so that each can live the beliefs most compatible with his or her own experience. Such a church would have only the two beliefs previously expressed: the sacredness of every individual, and the relativity of all beliefs. This line of thinking is inimical, however, to most churches today.

Why would one want to "join" a church with a creed of the relativity of all creeds? Precisely because he or she wants to be in a safe setting that allows intelligent, loving human beings to search, share and build together. What will they build? Whatever they decide to build. My bias would be to build cathedrals of human caring and sharing, so that, first of all, no child dies of hunger or disease, and every parent has the right and opportunity to earn a living by making their particular contribution on the planet. The point is, a church that is truly universal will be such, not because of any creed, but because it creates a context or vehicle for all people to grow spiritually.

From one point of view, this kind of church is not for everybody. That is, it is only for people who are secure enough to say: "I do realize that my beliefs are relative. I want to learn from others, as well as share with them. Perhaps together we can come up with something much better than I as an individual, or we, as an old style credo-bound church can come up with."

From another point of view, it is precisely this kind of church that is for everybody. It is a sort of shell church, which exploring Catholics or Lutherans or Jews or Muslims or any other believer could participate in. I find it hard to believe that many would, because it implies that they might "lose their own faith." I am afraid they would think that this church is one like theirs, one with a set of beliefs that you must subscribe to and profess in order to participate. It is very difficult – at least it was for me – to let go of the "absoluteness" of my beliefs and acknowledge their relativity. My fantasy is that slowly, gradually, we would all become part of one truly universal church that is called humanity, one in which all could share and learn from others, and work together to create a world that works for everyone. Since I am fantasizing, why not have it happen immediately instead of gradually!

2. Current churches don't create a world that works for everyone

Many churches are supposed to save the world, but they don't. When I speak of "saving the world," I am talking about saving <u>this</u> world, about ending hunger, poverty, environmental degradation and population growth. No secular institution has the vision, purpose or capability of creating a world that works for everyone. However, no <u>particular</u> church seems to fulfill, or be designed to fulfill, this role either. Although they purport to care about others in the world, many stand in judgment against them.

To understand why we need an all-inclusive church, we need to go back to how the human mind operates. Each of us thinks within the context of our own experience. That is, we draw from our past in order to explain the present and prepare for the future. We bring whatever mental resources we have to any problem or situation, and thus, if forced to, we can invent the resolution to any problem. If I asked you to write an essay on how to end world hunger, you could come up with something. However, the value of what you had to say would depend on the depth and breadth of your experience, information and beliefs. Most individual answers would be inadequate to resolve the problem. Most churches with a specific mandatory credo would also be inadequate. But, together, we could all come up with something that would resolve it.

I do not bring up the problem of hunger lightly. To resolve it requires precisely that we pool our mental resources to get as accurate a picture as possible of what is so, what needs to be done, and how to do it. Likewise, concerning spiritual belief, perhaps we are just as woefully inadequate. An alternative would be to admit that, yes, we do have some information, and yes, we do have some beliefs, but we are also willing to acknowledge their relativity so that we can learn from and share with others. That's the kind of church that is needed now.

The challenge of a new church

For an inclusive church there seem to be two inherent, big problems right off the bat: For the group that this church is most meant to appeal to, those who have dropped their traditional religious beliefs and are searching, or for those who have no uses for churches at all, the word "church" will have negative connotations. They don't want anything to do with formal, organized religions. On the other hand, the people who still have strong religious beliefs and who are happy with their current church will see such a church as a threat. It will seem to be just another kook fringe group.

This leaves us between a rock and a hard place. If the idea of "church" would alienate both of these groups – which is virtually everybody – why even use the term? Because most other concepts aren't large enough to encompass what is needed. A therapy group, life skills group, social betterment group, lifelong education group, etc. are too narrow in scope. Most of these groups don't have what I consider the fundamental purpose of a church. They don't enable each person to get in touch with the sacred within themselves and all around them, to fully express their spirituality, which is the same as to fully express their humanity. Secular movements, if they did take on what I propose, wouldn't really be secular. Or, better said, they would redefine the meaning of secular to include the spiritual as well. However, we now let the established churches maintain their monopoly on "spirituality" and waste vast amounts of human resources. We can't afford to do that. Someone needs to redeem spirituality from the churches!

If we are to create a structure of fulfillment that in fact creates a world that works for everyone, we have to play at the deepest possible level. We cannot heal ourselves as individuals and we cannot heal the planet unless we form a universal community. It is a very new way of interpreting what a church should be, or maybe more accurately, the resurrecting of a very old way.

None of what I have said is to detract from the ministers of current churches. They are some of the best people I know. They are intelligent, loving and hard-working. But they are trapped in a structure that isn't designed to work optimally to fulfill its ultimate purpose.

Summary

Current churches don't work optimally for individuals (a world that works for me), and they are not structured to create a world that works for everyone. This is because they generally are exclusive, not inclusive, by their very nature. First, despite the value that current churches do offer their members, they generally do not free people; they bind them into belief systems which at best are 20% useful and at worst cause people to kill each other. Secondly, current churches can't save the world. When I speak of "saving the world," I am talking about saving this world, about ending hunger, poverty, environmental degradation and population growth. The purpose of a church ought to be to create a world that works for everyone. Because many are trapped in their belief systems, they aren't equipped to do this.

Chapter 35:

THE GREAT FAILURE #2: HOW SECULAR INSTITUTIONS FAIL

There are several secular models of human organizations today, but all of these are inadequate to do the job of creating a world that works for me and for everyone. That is because it is not their job. Here are some of them.

1. Government – Theoretically, at least, the purpose of a democratic government is to create a nation that works for everyone in the nation. But it is ponderously slow and not too effective in a democratic nation, not to mention a non-democratic one. Most people who govern seem to be more interested in power and control than benevolence. Perhaps that is because the primary purpose of government seems to be defense or protection: people bind together to maintain their security by protecting themselves from an external enemy. Defense budgets in most industrialized countries, especially the U.S., and even in most Third World countries are the highest expenditure category. Anything can be justified if it is for "defense." This purpose necessarily focuses governments on their own well-being, not that of the whole world. The con-

cept of "global citizen" is still in its infancy. In addition, even within the U.S., <u>which</u> government are we talking about: national, state, county, city? Each jurisdiction has its own concern. Whose job is it to create a world that works for everyone? My city council? My mayor? My county board of supervisors? My state assembly representative? My state senator? My governor? My congressional representative? My senator? My President?

In addition, most nations still aren't even <u>nominally</u> democratic. Even if they were, it is going to take a long time before we actually have one democratic government for the whole world. We don't have time to wait.

2.   Businesses or The Corporation – The purpose of a business is to create a profit by providing particular goods or services. The purpose is not, nor can it be, to create a world that works for everyone. Businesses work on the premise that they have to compete for scarce resources. Putting your competitor out of business is viewed as good. Downsizing and eliminating as many jobs as possible is good. Externalizing your costs to society by getting tax breaks, polluting and so on is good. More profit is always better. For more about this, read David Korten's *When Corporations Rule the World.* Can you imagine a business with its purpose to create a world that works for everyone?

On the other hand, a novel way of looking at a new church is that we are creating a giant, non-profit corporation of 7 billion well-paid members. That means everybody in the world would be a member and would be taken care of – because they earn enough to take care of themselves. (I am being optimistic in thinking world population could level off at seven billion.) Not that people couldn't play the current game of business, the game of accumulation, but that they would recognize it as a game and would use the profits to get all seven billion into the fold. This is, of course, hard to imagine because when money is involved, the need for power and profit dominates – or at least seems to have.

3. Schools, Educational Institutions – Part of the purpose of a new church is to provide on-going education for the real world. I don't even like the word education. I prefer calling it ongoing personal growth and development – self-actualization, even. That should be the purpose of schools and educational institutions as well. Yet, most don't do that. The first reason is that school lasts only for 8 or 12 or 16 or 18 years, thankfully. Learning is life long. Some adult education programs partially answer to that. But there is a deeper issue of why schools can't work.

   Most schools, including adult education programs that are not specifically for skill training, are trapped in this paradigm: they all focus on "subjects" rather than "the subject," the person who is supposed to be educated. This leads to fragmentation. Nobody educates the whole person. It's nobody's responsibility. My job is to teach you English. Her job is to teach you math. His job is to teach you biology. Nobody's job is to educate the whole person. By default, they focus from top down, and from outside in. That is, teachers still tell students rather than draw out from students. They try to pour information in rather than draw information out. There are very few, if any, educational institutions that are student–centered, such as problem-based learning (PBL) programs at several universities, where student and teachers alike explore their own needs — who they are, what they want, what they want to know, where they are going. None do it on a life-long basis. Yet, "the kingdom of god is within."

4. Service organizations – Many groups like Rotary, Kiwanis, Lions, etc. do good works for society. For example, Rotary has made the commitment to supply all the polio vaccine needed to end polio in the world. What an immense good work! However, from how I see these groups operate, they seem to function primarily as social or networking clubs. I believe the glue that holds them together and keeps them going is the specific services they are committed to. In my experi-

ence, groups that simply focus on socializing or self-help by themselves, don't seem to hold together. One socializes with those he feels comfortable with. And that shifts, depending on circumstances. But a group with an outer-directed goal seems to function better. Even when service organizations do this, they don't take on the whole world. They take on a piece of the puzzle, but not the whole puzzle. Who takes on creating a world that works for everyone?

5. Seminar or motivational affiliation groups, such as Landmark – these have no permanent glue except the growth of the individual and extending the organization. Many seminars help individuals focus on works of community service, which is great. Yet, these seem to be splintered efforts rather than coordinated and sustainable action. Once the individual doesn't want to take any more seminars, or doesn't want to support people coming into the seminars, then there is not much motivation to stay involved.

6. Charities, non-profit organizations – Charities are similar to all of the groups above. They focus on one particular aspect of creating a world that works for everyone, but they don't take responsibility for the whole. As you read this, you may be saying, "If you want to create a world that works for everyone, of course you have to break it down into pieces. Who can do it all?" That is true, but unfortunately groups often lose sight of the goal of a world that works for everyone, and we become insular in the work we are doing. Unfortunately, some even lose sight of their primary objective. Non-profits sometimes become bureaucracies with the goal of self- preservation. It is interesting to see how the administrative expenses of some charities creep up and the expenditures for their specific work go down. It is also interesting to see how the salaries of the chief administrator seem to grow as well. Of course, the objective of any charity should be to put themselves out of business. That is, if your goal is to help the homeless, your overall objective should be to end

homelessness, period. (Homelessness, by the way, is a false distinction. Being homeless is a symptom of a deeper problem. We really need to be looking at what can we do to help those with mental illness, those with substance abuse problems, broken families and so on.)

7. Human Care Professions – the frustrating thing to me is that all of the health professions seem to be fragmented as well. Each – doctors, psychologists, body healers, chiropractors, nutritionists, acupuncturists, etc. – think they know 100% of what it takes for a person to be healthy and whole. Doctors think they know everything but they really know only 10%. Chiropractors know only 10% and so do all the others. Yet, how many of them talk to each other? In my experience, most seem to disdain each other. I had the idea of making a deal with doctors: "I'll pay you a small fee, and if you can cure this problem, I'll pay your whole fee. That way, I don't take all of the risk. You risk something as well." But of course, this would not go over well with doctors or any of the professions. Why? It would be an admission that possibly they didn't know everything, that their business was partially experimental – as all life is. It would challenge their income, their self-preservation. So, each profession is forced to pretend that they know everything and not open themselves up to any new learning. They are inevitably trapped within their own paradigms. The "holistic practitioners," those who try to incorporate learning from all professions, are not given credence because they don't have the "in-depth knowledge" that other professions have.

No secular institution takes on, or can take on, a world that works for everyone. No one can do everything, so we specialize. And then we become fragmented. Being fragmented means that we lose our organic wholeness. All of the parts of an organism have specialized functions, yet they must work in coordination with the whole. Losing sight of the big picture seems to be endemic for all organizations, secular and religious. Self-preservation seems to be the corrupter of many organizations. What would it take for the human community to stay focused on a world that works for everyone, and not fragment into self-serving splinters?

Since current institutions don't have a focus of creating a world that works for everyone, what is the answer? It is a new kind of church, an overarching community that has as its specific purpose to help individuals continue to grow at their deepest level <u>and</u> to stop at no less a goal than a world that works for everyone. It might infuse all of the institutions listed above with the big picture and link us into one organic whole. Even given people's old paradigm of an outie god, if we spent all of our time ignoring him and just healed and prospered the planet and ourselves, do you think he would mind? No; when we get to heaven he will say, "When you did it for the least of my brethren, you did it for me." The surprise, the shocking revelation of those words of Jesus, is that being a Christian is not going to get you into heaven. Jesus talks about people arriving at heaven's gate and the Father welcomes them in because he says, "When I was hungry you gave me to eat; when I was thirsty you gave me to drink." They say, "When did we do this for you?" He answers, "When you did it for the least of my brothers, you did it for me." The astonishing thing is that they didn't know they were doing it for god or Jesus, they just did it for the person they did it for! They weren't "trying to get to heaven" or "being Christian." What should be shocking about this to Christians is that if you are trying to be a Christian, you don't get into heaven. The Muslims, Jews, pagans, epicureans, etc. who feed the hungry, give drink to the thirsty are the ones who are going to make it!

This is my vision and the next chapter tells how such a church would operate.

Summary

Current secular institutions such as government, business, etc. are not structured to create a world that works for everyone. This overarching goal requires something less insular than any secular organization.

Chapter 36:

HOW WOULD A UNIVERSAL CHURCH OPERATE?

What might a church that has as its purpose to create a world that works for everyone look like? How would it operate?

On the following pages I outline some of my thoughts on how it would be structured. One of the values of such a church is to empower people in other churches. In other words, you don't have to "leave" your church to belong to this one. In fact, it would be great if a group of Catholics, for example, formed a support group in this church, and then used it to empower their own church. If that is too threatening, they could just pretend this new church was not really a church! What if groups of ministers got together in support groups so that they could tackle burn-out, or have a safe forum where they could express their doubts, air their questions and so on? If you are in a church now, feel free to steal any ideas that would work for you!

I have to confess that I feel very strange in this final edit. I seem to present a very clear picture of what a universal church might look like. I phrase things as if it already exist. At the same time I am not compelled to do anything about starting one...the universe is unfolding as it should!

Mission Statement

The mission of this church is to create a world that works for everyone. For individuals we provide an ongoing forum of support to explore and pursue our spiritual and personal growth – a world that works for me. For mankind we marshal human energy to resolve critical global problems and create a global community – a world that works for everyone.

Beliefs

We believe:

1. Each individual is sacred. We all share in divinity.
2. All beliefs are relative, not absolute (including these two).

Agreements

As members we agree to:

1. Get value out of our participation
2. Give value to others

Spiritual Rules

There are no "rules" to follow. Rather, each of us must formulate our own "rules" for life. Rules are not prescriptions of how I "must" act, but descriptions of how I act when am my truest self. They are natural outflow of who I am.

Some of my own personal current affirmations or "rules," if you happen to like that word are:

1. I respect the sacredness of every person.

- I honor the divinity, wonder, vitality, power within me and every person.

- I reverence myself and each person I meet for their magnificence, their great potential and for what they can and do contribute.
- I reverence my feelings, intuitions, desires. I allow my deepest desires to come forth, because it is there that I make my deepest contribution and fully express my uniqueness.
- I am joyful.
- My presence and interactions spread joy in the universe.

2. I acknowledge the power and the relativity of all beliefs, including mine.

- I never let beliefs get in the way of reverencing others.
- I allow and assist others in sharing and challeng ing their beliefs, so that I learn from them and they learn from me.
- I share but don't impose my beliefs.

Membership

To be a member of the church, a person agrees to get and give value through their participation. This means the member will regularly evaluate whether he or she is getting value and giving value, and, if not, to either modify their participation so that they do or leave the church. If they are not getting or giving value, they are, de facto, not a member. Of course, they are free to rejoin at any moment by re-making these agreements.

"Services"/Events

I believe that one of the most powerful tools that such a church would use is the internet. How it would do that is not totally clear to me right now. However, two things are clear. First, if people want to make a difference in creating a world that works for everyone, the internet has abundant information on how to do so, and who is doing it. Secondly, people with similar needs can easily link through this medium.

More importantly, such a community would also provide and participate in external events. These might be called "services" in old church talk, but they wouldn't resemble them very much. I envision that members would participate in one or more of the following four different types of "services," or events, each month:

1. Spiritual/Personal Growth (SPG) Group

The primary event which I see as paramount is a Spiritual/Personal Growth Group (SPG). These support groups of four to six of the same individuals meets once (or more) monthly at a mutually convenient time and place to discuss their spiritual/personal growth. If the universe is an intelligent, vital force that continues to evolve, each of us has that force within ourselves. We need to explore what that life force calls for in each stage of our life.

In the **Growing Up** chapter, I suggested that we need to pull back and examine our beliefs. The SPG is a safe place to do that. It enables each person to share their current concerns, questions, goals. Each member has the commitment to get and give value. Personal goal-setting and accountability might be part of what these groups do. The metaphor that Jesus used was that where two or three were gathered in his name, he would be in the midst of them.

The intention is that each person would get so much value out of this group that they would want to share the format with others by voluntarily going out to create and mentor a new SPG group. This is much like how the root system of a honeysuckle plant expands (See "Honeysuckle Church" in the **Possible Names for a New Church** chapter.) The need for the SPG group will be further discussed in the next chapter.

2. Spiritual/Personal Growth Forum

In this forum, one of the members or an outside speaker speaks on and discusses a topic of spiritual/personal growth each month. An integral part of this event is members breaking out into groups of four to six people to discuss personal reactions and thoughts relating to the talk. These are preferably with members who are not in a person's SPG Group, so as not to create insularity.

3. Social Action Forum

This is the forum that focuses on the question of what it will take to create a world that works for everyone. Experts or informed members speak on a social issue – poverty, population, environment, etc. – including opportunities on how to participate to resolve that issue. Individuals then break out into groups of four to six to discuss the issue and their potential participation in resolving it. They also share about their personal ongoing efforts to create a world that works for everyone, in the whatever sphere of contribution they are focusing on.

Each member is active in some action to forward society, to create a world that works for everyone. Each of us needs to explore and express something bigger than ourselves. I want no less than the end of poverty on our planet. I want a world without war. I want our schools to stop stifling and start empowering children. I want no one living on the streets. There is a big agenda of opportunity out there to make a difference.

We are so busy in our day-to-day pursuits, that it is difficult to look at the bigger picture. Some of us are moved by love or guilt or both to do some kind of community service, but often it is token action. Or, we contribute a few dollars to organizations periodically to be able to say, "At least I did something." Consistent, sustained, effective action to change this seems to be a rare commodity. Perhaps the church would give IGOMFA awards to people: I got off my fat ass!

4. Spiritual/Personal Growth Workshops

Series of workshops can be held on topics of personal and spiritual growth. The purpose is to heal the past and to energize our human and spiritual potential for the future. They are in the areas that seem to pre-occupy most people, and which need to be handled so that people can get on with using their energies to create a world that works for everyone. The topics and needs are developed by members. They would be on the "business of life": time, money, health, relationships, right livelihood, parenting, marriage, etc. These topics can also obviously be discussed in the monthly SPG group meetings described above. Both of these events enable members to engage in personal life-long learning.

These last three types of events could easily be combined as members saw fit. Each of these events would involve feedback to the organizers – perhaps a written evaluation – so they know to what degree the event is giving value to participants.

Summary

A truly universal church has the purpose of creating a world that works for the individual and a world that works for everyone. Some possible characteristics of such a church are listed in this chapter.

Chapter 37:

WHY DO WE NEED SPIRITUAL/PERSONAL GROWTH GROUPS?

"Life is a daring adventure, or it is nothing at all," said Helen Keller. The challenge is to live life at a sustained level of vitality, daring. If indeed god is a metaphor for the intelligent, loving/gracious, beautiful, forward-thrusting energy/life force of/in atoms, stars, creatures, people, the universe, then it would pay to periodically re-evaluate my role in this process. It seems to me that there are two over-arching challenges that prevent us from doing so:

- We need to constantly pull ourselves back from the level of the mundane, from the tyranny of the urgent, from the business of getting and spending, from raising children, from the thousands of necessities that creep into this petty pace from day to day unto the last syllables of recorded time. (I'm sorry; I got carried away!) We forget who we are, our sacredness, our innate divinity. We forget that we have something unique and powerful to offer. All of the daily activities are part of who we are, but not unless we recognize that they are and pursue those activities in context and in balance.
- We need to pull ourselves up when we fall, when we

227

have setbacks, when we are ill — physically, psychologically or spiritually — when we have gone one step
forward and two steps backwards, when confronted
with the negatives of life. I sometimes think the measure of success in life is: how fast can you recover?

Because of these, we need to pull ourselves back regularly
to seek the divine in ourselves and others. The word "religion" comes from two Latin roots, "re" and "ligio" which
mean to "bind back." Reflection, etymologically, means to
"bend back." That is what church-going is supposed to do
for us, bring us back to our divine life force, our truest self.
So the fundamental activity of this church is to get together
in small groups once a month to talk about ourselves. We
need to discover and uncover the spiritual and divine in
ourselves, to discover and uncover our relation with the
world and the contribution we want to make to it. We need
to explore the changes we are going through: where do
we get stopped, what needs healing, what's next for us?
We also need to have goals, to remind ourselves of them,
to renew them, or change them. We need to get back in
touch with our fundamental values. We need to have a
vision of what our life is about and to rediscover, reassert
and expand that vision. We don't really need anybody to
tell us what vision, values or goals we should have. Primarily, we just need to look into ourselves to elicit them.
However, the questions, comments and listening of others may play a vital role in opening up new doors for us,
in shifting our paradigms. As we share ourselves with others, we inspire them to open up to who they are as well.

Even though some churches seem to acknowledge these
needs, the way churches are structured stems from a cen-
turies-old paradigm. So the context determines the content, even though they may claim that the content is different. What I mean is that unless each person is engaged
in self-exploration and self-expression at each gathering,
a church is not delivering full value. When does one ever
get the chance to explore their beliefs, explore their puzzle-
ments, questions, doubts? When do we get to ask sincere
questions of others, because we want to learn from them?

When do we actually acknowledge that each of us is sacred, so all we need to do to understand sacredness is to look at and express what is within? This is why we need a whole new context for a church service or event. Creation is happening constantly, so we need an on-going opportunity to explore and participate in it.

What Does Spiritual/Personal Growth Mean?

In trying to have the name of the Support Group describe its purpose, I use the words "Spiritual" and "Personal." In truth, I find it hard to make a distinction between the two. As I see it, when you take care of yourself, when you take care of your growth in any way, you are being spiritual. When our physical and emotion needs are taken care of, then we are freed up to pursue our deeper spiritual needs. This doesn't necessarily happen sequentially, because we need to take care of our physical needs, our emotional needs, our intellectual needs, and our spiritual needs at the same time. Yet, as with Maslow's hierarchy of needs, one need generally takes precedence over the others at any given time. When we fulfill one need, we fulfill all because we are a unit. So I have the confidence that when people are seeking to grow, seeking what's next for them, it is always a spiritual quest. It leads them into expressing who they uniquely are.

This means that any issue regarding one's personal growth is up for discussion at a meeting: one's health, relationships, money, work, time, parenting, goals, spiritual questions, worries, etc. People need to get value at whatever level they are currently focused on. They need to discuss what is on their mind. The more profoundly integrated we become, the more profound contribution we can make to others. Whatever affects us – either what is holding us back or what we need to look at for our next level of growth – is spiritual.

However, the discussion should focus on growth, rather than just chatting or reporting. It is the responsibility of each individual to get value out of their participation, and this is generally commensurate with the amount of risk they are willing to take in opening themselves to others. All members of the group need to monitor the discussion to make sure that people are getting value. This is why the group should periodically take its temperature, that is, evaluate the degree to which individuals are benefiting or growing.

The word "growth" connotes "adding on," but I suggest a different way of looking at it. In our early years our bodies grow by adding on. Our mind grows by adding information. But in adulthood, the most important growth has to do not so much with adding on but with "taking off." Even on the physical level, growth for most adults means ironically taking off – taking off weight, taking toxic substances out of the body, etc. Once we have reached a mature state in our body, health generally means keeping it in balance and in integrity. Most of us don't do that because we eat too much, we eat the wrong kinds of foods, and we don't exercise enough. So, growth in the body means shedding pounds and toxins and flabbiness so that we can function in a healthy, happy manner. Likewise, growth on the intellectual level means shedding old concepts. We get stuck in paradigms of thinking. In order to grow, we have to adopt new paradigms, look at things in a new way. Likewise, on the emotional level, growth really means looking at what really blocks us from moving forward. All of us have addictive behaviors. We have attitudes that are built into us from our parents, peer groups and to a great extent our genes. We are prone towards certain things. Some of these things are not in our best interest, e.g., alcoholism.

Personal growth means focusing our attention in two ways. First, we need to explore and clarify our goals and intentions. What do we want out of life? Where are we going? What quality of life are we looking for? Once we decide where we are going, the next question is: How do we get there? These questions help us to formulate the big picture. The SPG group gives us the opportunity to pull back from the tyranny of the urgent and to focus on the where we are going and what prevents us from getting there. When people have a safe environment for speaking, magic happens. The better we feel about ourselves and our own growth, the more we become peaceful, attuned to our role in the universe, and able to fulfill that role. That is what spiritual means: attuning ourselves to our larger role in the universe, and to actually invent that role.

Why is the SPG Group the Most Important Church Activity?

God, in the outie sense, doesn't play favorites. She is concerned about the welfare of every creature. You are no more or less important then any of your six billion brothers and sisters. How does the old saying go: "You are a child of the universe, no less than the trees and the stars. You have a right to be here." There is only one person in the universe who has an inside track on taking care of your spiritual/personal growth. Pay attention to yourself once in a while. That's why an SPG Group is of paramount importance.

In addition, the SPG Group is the church's most important activity because we can't create a world that works for everyone until we create a world that works for ourselves first. Until you see the dignity and magnificence of yourself as a human being and the privilege of being here, you cannot offer what's deepest and most important to others. Not that you spend 90 years getting your own act together, and then you look out to the rest of the world. We have to focus on ourselves and the world at the same time. Neither job can be adequately done without the other. An SPG group works in tandem with the Social Action Forum/Group. The first focuses on a world that works for me, and the second on a world that works for everyone. When I think about crime, mislead youth, poverty, addiction in the U.S., not to mention wars and global PPE mentioned earlier, I ask, "How are we ever going to resolve these problems unless we have an abundance of order in our own lies, unless we feel good about ourselves and the direction we are moving in, unless we have our own health and finances and relationships in order? We need our own ongoing life skills taken care of, so that we can continue to reach out to others in more meaningful ways. We need to do both at the same time. You can't impoverish yourself to end the poverty of others; you can't enrich yourself unless you are ending the poverty of others.

When I speak of taking care of our needs, I mean all of them at the same time: physical, emotional, intellectual, and spiritual needs. However, one need generally takes precedence over the others at any given time. Maslow's hierarchy of needs explains this well. If people are at a level where they have physical pain, disability, or illness, that's what needs to be taken care of first. So maybe people spend two or three years just working on their physical well-being. After that, people need to work on the positive side of physical well-being, to provide themselves food, shelter, and clothing. So a homeless person would have to find out what he needs to do to get food and shelter on a regular basis. (When I was a Christian Brother the initials of the Order which we used after our names were "F.S.C." This stood for Fratres Scholarum Christianarum – Brothers of the Christian Schools – but we said that it meant "Food, Shelter and Clothing!") People may have to work on that level for a couple of years. Once people have food, shelter and clothing they move to the next level of need – security. When we have security that means we see that they have the capacity to generate a stream of income that will help support us and a fall back plan in case that stream dries up. If people are worried about their survival, they can't be worried about other people's survival. After these levels are handled the need for love comes in: reaching out to others and helping them have those same things that you have. Beyond that level is the level of esteem. What do I want to do so that I can be proud of myself and so that others will esteem me? Then the highest level is that of self-actualization. What is my unique genius, joy, love, gift. What is it that I uniquely can do that no one else can do or seems to be doing? As Buckie Fuller says, the things that need doing are the things that you see need to be done which nobody else seems to be doing and which you can do.

In summary, the purpose of the SPG Group is to support each person's growth in each of these levels so that they can more fully actualize themselves, become more fully and truly human, and make a greater and greater contribution to the rest of mankind. Creating a world that works for yourself and for others are mutually inclusive. You can't do one without the other. You can't heal yourself without healing the planet, and you can't heal the planet without healing yourself. Engaging in both of these enterprises – which is the natural outcome of appreciating the dignity, awe and wonder of yourself and therefore of others – is what constitutes spiritual growth.

In order to facilitate this growth, I 've outlined some general SPG Group guidelines which I think will powerfully aid the process. These are not rules. They can and should be changed by a SPG group if they don't support the needs of the group.

Spiritual/Personal Growth Group Guidelines

The purpose of the SPG Group is to explore and deepen our spiritual and personal growth, to explore and pursue our vision in life. Our presence in the group is a statement of our commitment to get and give value. We each take full responsibility to get and to give value. Here are some guidelines to facilitate that:

1. Meet for 2 hours at least once a month. Be on time. End on time.
2. Start by meditating silently for 2 or 3 minutes on how you would like to get and give value.
3. Spontaneously, or in order, have each person talk for at least 10 minutes. Others can freely interact.
4. Each person briefly shares about what has happened in their life since the last meeting and then what their current questions, issues, concerns are.
5. The purpose of the group is self-exploration, self-discovery, self-growth. Talk about society or external issues only inasmuch as it helps talk about yourself.
6. Appoint a group facilitator at each session whose job is to:
    • make sure everyone gets to talk for at least 10 minutes.
    • prevent individuals from dominating the discussion.

- prevent the conversation from degenerating into socializing or chatting rather than talking about ourselves.
- to monitor the time.

These are the on-going responsibilities of all group members, but a specific person should have the responsibility at each meeting.

7. Don't "fix" people. Let them discover their own answers and path. Ask questions caringly and abundantly. Give advice sparingly. However, sharing your own journey can be very useful to others (and yourself).

8. End by having each person say what they need to say to be complete and in what way they want to grow or what miracle they would like to have happen for them by the next meeting.

9. Do a periodic evaluation on how the group is doing: Give a rating (A, B, C, D or F) to the group on how useful or valuable it has been. Then discuss why you give it this rating and what it would take for you to give it an "A" rating.

10. Give out a good door prize. Just kidding - but it feels incomplete stopping at 9. Oh, I know: Each member will have the intention of getting such value out of the group that they will be very eager to start and monitor a satellite group, if appropriate for them.

I also want to share another set of group guidelines that echo my thoughts and include other useful ideas as well. They are from *The Co-Creators Handbook*, co-authored by Carolyn Anderson and Katharine Roske. You can see them on www.globalfamily.net.

The Co-Creator's Agreements

1. **Commit to the Mission**
   Our mission is to liberate ourselves and all humanity to realize our full potential. I agree to use this mission as a guide for my actions.

2. **Communicate with Integrity**
   I agree to tell my truth, with compassion for myself and others.

3. **Listen with Your Heart**
   I agree to listen respectfully to the communication of others and attune to their deepest meaning.

4. **Honor One Another**
   I agree to honor each person's process, acknowledging that everyone, including myself, is making the best possible choice or decision we are capable of at that moment of choice or decision.

5. **Appreciate Your Contributions**
   I agree to take responsibility for getting acknowledged.

6. **Express Appreciation for Others' Contributions**
   I agree to acknowledge others.

7. **Honor Our Differences**
   I agree to come from a sense of cooperation and caring in my interactions with others, and from an understanding that goals are often the same even though methods for achieving them may differ.

8. **Use Grievances as Opportunities to Evolve Self**
   I agree to look for the unresolved issue within me that creates a reaction to another's behavior.

9. **Maintain Resonance**
   I agree to take the time to establish rapport and then to re-connect with anyone with whom I feel out of harmony as soon as it's appropriate.

10. **Resolve Problems Constructively**
    I agree to offer at least one solution any time I present a problem. I agree to take problems, complaints and upsets to the person(s) with whom I can resolve them, at the earliest opportunity. I agree not to criticize or complain to someone who cannot do something about my complaint, and I will redirect others to do the same.

11. **Go For Excellence**
    I agree to support others and to be supported in participating at the highest level of excellence.

12. **Learn From Experience**
    I agree to look for opportunities to learn from my experiences, to continue doing what works and discontinue doing what does not work.

13. **Be a Leader**
    I agree to foster an environment of genuine collaboration, in which all people, including myself,

feel empowered to express our individual and collective potential.

14. **Re-evaluate Your Commitment**

    I agree to choose and re-choose to participate in this core group. It's my choice.

15. **Lighten UP!**

    I agree to create joy in my relationships, my work and my life.

The idea of a Spiritual/Personal Growth Group is, of course, not new. A few groups which I know of who already have established "core groups" are:

- The Foundation for Conscious Evolution. Organized by Barbara Marx Hubbard (Peaceroom.org). I am currently participating in a FCE core group.
- The Global Family, whose guidelines and web-site I just gave above.
- Renaissance Unity Alliance Sacred Circles, originated by Marianne Williamson (churchoftoday.com)

I am sure many others are available as well.

Summary

Because of the stress of modern life, we need to pull ourselves back regularly to seek the divine in ourselves and in others. That is the purpose of the Spiritual/Personal Support Group. When we take care of our personal growth – our physical, emotional, intellectual and spiritual needs – we are being spiritual. The SPG Group is the church's most important activity because we can't create a world that works for everyone until we create a world that works for ourselves first. Not that you spend 90 years getting your own act together, and then look out to the rest of the world. We have to focus on ourselves and the world at the same time. Neither job can be adequately fulfilled without the other. I've included some guidelines on how such a group might operate.

Chapter 38:

LEADERSHIP IN THE CHURCH

Who will lead the church?

Leadership

Leaders in a church are not "appointed" but emerge naturally. As one student I taught many years ago said, "respect should be commanded, not demanded." Leaders will emerge naturally by the power of their character, speech and action. The best kind of leaders are those who create a space for others to flourish. They facilitate growth.

I have two beliefs concerning leaders. First, when people slavishly stick to a charismatic leader, they also bless the flaws of that leader as well — their lack of knowledge, lack of insight, and lack of experience. They deify people like Jesus, Mohammed, and Buddha and actually do a disservice to them and the rest of mankind. My second and more important belief is that although these leaders were certainly charismatic, every person on the planet has charisma. Charisma means "a special gift." Everyone on the planet has a special gift. Everyone has unique genes, comes from a unique background and therefore has something unique to offer the rest of the world. From this belief, it follows that a church can be entrusted to the people who constitute it. We need to find a way that we can elicit what's best in every person and minimize their flaws. As Peter

237

Drucker said, "Never promote a manager who doesn't make mistakes," and, "build on people's strengths." It's too much of a burden for any leader to understand everything, make all decisions, and have all data in mind. But when we as a community regularly converse, share what we know and what we don't know, then we can make much better decisions and forward the progress of mankind.

Mankind only progresses because we communicate – share what we know, and better yet, what we don't know. Communication is what makes us "cum unus," makes us "one with" the rest of mankind. So the progress of the planet and the church depends on communication. Everyone is the leader because everyone gets to communicate. This kind of leadership creates a free and open church, one that can evolve as the insights of mankind evolve. It eliminates worry about the lunatic fringe. The Hitlers of the world can join this church. But because everyone has the opportunity to share ideas openly, the Jesus', Moses', Mohammeds, Buddhas of the world will prevail. A better way of saying this is that in an atmosphere of open communication, the better side of us will win out over the worse side.

It goes without saying that the internet is a powerful tool for communicating.

Finances

I have some thoughts about how money should operate in a church. Most of them come about in reaction to what now happens in churches.

- I am inclined to side with the early Paul who felt that none of the leaders of the early Christian church should do it for a living; that is, they don't make money from doing it. Leaders should be gainfully employed, and do this work part-time, or be independently wealthy and do it full-time if they choose. Of course, since this is a democratic church, if a specific community votes to support a leader, that is their right. This supports the other side of the issue: a laborer is worthy of her pay. However, my purpose in saying that leaders should not rely on the church to make a living is so that nothing get in the way of its spreading to serve all mankind. That is, neither the spreader (knowing he has to make his home mortgage payment this month) nor the "spreadees" (wondering whether personal gain might be the motivation of the spreader) should get in the way of the spreading. I wonder whether Paul <u>continued</u> to be a tent-maker!

- Another reason for having leaders make a contribution without having to make a living from it is that some of us have a tremendous amount to give others on a professional level. That's what doctors, lawyers, teachers, healers, etc. do. However, the fact that they have to charge fees for their work binds them. Participating in the church will free them because it will allow them to share their wisdom on a personal rather than professional basis. That means that if they are not charging you money for services, they are free to explore with you rather than prescribe for you. They become free to admit that they don't have all the answers. They don't have to be defensive about what they're saying because they are not charging you for it. This is very freeing for both. They can consider what they contribute as an experiment.

- Each group has to be self-sufficient. So, if they rent a hall for their meeting, they should pay for it, and if they have a secretary coordinating E-mailings, etc., then he/she should be paid a fair wage. Those who present Spiritual/Personal Growth Workshops should be compensated based on contributions of attendees. These workshops on specific topics are presented by someone versed in the area, so they should be compensated. Perhaps this would be a fixed percent of the revenue from those workshops.

- Very little money should be invested in brick and mortar. The other churches are all excellent at doing that, and their buildings lie fallow for the large majority of the week. Something like Tuesday night could be the "Sabbath day." Then just rent from other churches when they are empty. Or rent churches on Saturday and synagogues on Sunday or mosques on both!

- People should have the opportunity to contribute financially to the church. This is for three reasons:

  1) If people get value out of their participation, then they should give value. One way humans ac knowledge value is through money. People can ask: What level of regular financial contribution to the church adequately expresses the value I receive, and what am I able to contribute at this point in my life?
  2) Money is needed to fund any enterprise.
  3) If we are serious about creating a world that works for everyone, we will invest in those who are do ing that. One thought is that the church would au tomatically contribute half of any money taken in to a group that is working to end war, or hunger, or homelessness, etc. When money is involved, an organization can get too self-centered in its own growth or survival and lose sight of its purpose. Committing 50% of contributions off the top com mits us to a world that works for everyone. In this case, whether or not individuals or groups get caught up in being too self-centered, the financial commitment to the rest of the world is always there and always happening.

Summary

Leaders will not be appointed but will emerge naturally. Money should serve the mission of the church, not impede it. I include a few thoughts above on money in the church.

Chapter 39:

POSSIBLE NAMES FOR A NEW CHURCH

What might such a church be named? At different times I have thought of various names for a church, each of which captures some of the flavor of what I envision. I will share them with you to express the underlying vision that the name suggests. These are, of course, in addition to the subtitles I listed earlier, and the dozens of names graciously suggested by participants in my workshops.

1. Church of the Saviors of This World

The name *Church of the Saviors of This World* means that we are not trying to do anything for the next world, if there should happen to be one, but we acknowledge that <u>this</u> is the world that needs saving. I spoke of the PPE problems earlier. Population is still booming. Hunger is still rampant. Pollution is still rampant. We industrialized countries are still depleting global natural resources with abandon. Wars abound. This world, this planet is what needs saving. More importantly, it is lives in this world that must be saved. One billion people are still malnourished and live from hand to mouth everyday. Their lives literally need to be saved. Saving needs to happen here and now, not as some pie in the sky later.

And who is going to do the saving? One person? Of course not, we must all do it together. If we don't do it, nobody will. It is as simple as that. We are all co-creators, part of evolution. So, anyone participating in this church automatically commits to saving the world in whatever fashion they can. The more people who commit to it, the more unified the effort, and the more quickly we resolve these problems. It galls me to hear pseudo-Christians using Jesus' words, "You shall always have the poor with you," as an excuse to do nothing.

2. Church of The Seekers and Finders

The name *Church of the Seekers and Finders* acknowledges that we are all seekers and finders at the same time. Those who participate are seeking their personal and spiritual growth. At the same time, it demonstrates that we are all finders. That is, we all have reached a certain level of success in living, have found ways of being that serve us, have found answers. By the very fact that we are alive, we have all "made it." At least we have made it to this point here and now. No one is lacking. We are successful at the game of life. There may be more that we want in life, but we need to acknowledge that we have been successful in bringing ourselves this far and maintaining ourselves where we are. We are "found"; we stand on a found-ation.

On the other hand, as seekers, we are all looking for something. There are two kinds of seekers. The first kind is the seeker who lacks something. Their life is not satisfactory. Something is missing. They are in pain or they are unhappy or perhaps they just feel empty. They don't have a sense of fulfillment, a sense of satisfaction, a sense that everything is fine just the way it is. They may have a sense that their life doesn't have meaning. They may just be uncomfortable about being a human speck on a planetary speck in a brief moment of time and wondering if this is all that there is, because it doesn't seem to be enough for them.

The second kind of seeker is one who has pretty much resolved past issues and is satisfied with the present. They have a sense of satisfaction in their lives. They have the sense, "If I died today it would be okay. My life is fulfilled.

There is nothing wanting in my life." They are those that have arrived, the illuminati. So, their search is not one that comes out of any lack. It is one that comes out of abundance, "I have an abundant life now and I am just looking at what is next. How can I do more, be more, achieve more, make more of a difference?" And yet, none of these is necessary for a sense of satisfaction about themselves. They are finders who are seeking for what's next.

Even though we are all seekers in one of the two senses above, we are still a church of people who are masters rather than victims in our lives. A victim in life is someone who doesn't really believe that they share in divinity, that they are sacred, that they have the power to create simply because they choose to. The master mentality means I can be godlike at any moment, raise myself out of any adversity and take the next step in creating a fuller existence for myself. People who are victims have no faith in the divine because they have no faith in themselves. They don't acknowledge the magnificence of existence and the magnificence of the privilege of being on the planet and being a co-creator of its future. An outie god, by the way, doesn't care what stance you take. It is just that you lose out on your life if you choose to be a victim.

A church of seekers and finders, then, is a group of people who acknowledge that they are both, and who have both something to offer others and something to learn from others. At a Spiritual/Personal Growth Forum any member who had something significant to say could give the "sermon." In fact, if the group met 52 times a year there might be 52 different sermon givers. Imagine how much energy would be freed up if preachers and pastors didn't have to make up a sermon every Sunday – the energy of both the preacher and the congregation!

3. The Honeysuckle Church

Another name might be *The Honeysuckle Church*. This comes from the thought that growth should happen sweetly, naturally and organically, like that of a honeysuckle plant or any living organism.

243

Here is how I came up with the honeysuckle concept. Our street is on a hillside, so the houses on it are tiered. I was looking at the hillside between my house and the one above and noticed that the honeysuckle vine had crept down the fence and was taking over the hillside. I decided to pull it out so that the ground cover we planted would spread better. I figured that it would take me about an hour to do the job. It took over four hours! Here's why: when you pull up one plant, it is not just one plant. Each plant seemed to have five or six branches going out from it which spread out and root themselves. Each new rooting then has five or six extensions which spread out and root, and so on. So, it is not as if you are pulling up one plant at a time; you have to pull up a whole network of plants.

It seems to me that this is the way a church should operate. The foundation is a group of five or six people. Why five or six? Not just because of the honeysuckle but because to share more than superficially about their lives takes time. Larger groups don't work. A group of five or six is intimate, and yet diverse enough to have a variety of input. It also is like the Grameen Bank model where you have many tiny little banks formed by five people but linked together in one huge network.

The second part of the honeysuckle concept that I like is that it spreads naturally, with one plant shooting out to create several more. That is how a church or any powerful movement spreads, organically and from within. When people see the value they get from their group they naturally go out and form another group. These groups would form a huge network, all with the goal of getting and giving value.

4. The catholic Church

Note the small "c" above. I am just being facetious about this name. Of course, it could never be named that because, other than trademark laws and the confusion it would cause, this "catholic" church might even be considered "anti-Catholic!" The original meaning of "catholic" is "universal." Without getting into the merits of whether the Catholic Church is that, my vision is of a truly universal church, which would even include Catholics!

I was in a support group of devout Christians (except for myself) a while back, and they took strong exception to my suggesting that we call our group a "church." To them it would mean supplanting their Christian church. My thought was that it would not supplant but support it. If people's faith empowers them, I don't want to take it away. I want to reinforce it. And when I say "empowers," I mean that it gives meaning to their life, helps them grow and helps them to reach out to others. When a faith does that, I support it 100%.

A truly universal church would support all people, meaning that it would support a multiplicity of beliefs. So, as I said earlier, the perfect church would be composed of Catholics, Jews, atheists, Muslims, etc. Anyone who believed in the sacredness of every individual and therefore the relativity of all beliefs, could participate. If a person didn't believe that all beliefs were relative – for example, that their Christian belief was absolute – why would they want to have anything to do with this church? Because it is a vehicle for getting and giving value. It would link them with a federation whose purpose is to create a world that works for themselves and for everyone. They could form their own Christian SPG Group. They could explore and strengthen their Christianity. Likewise for Judaism, Buddhism, etc.

My fervent desire is that all churches steal ideas from the format I have outlined, especially the Spiritual/Personal Support Group idea, so that they can more powerfully support and strengthen their members. I suspect that even this would be to threatening to established churches, even if they did it within their own church. Who knows, maybe a few will see the value in this kind of structure. Please feel free to use any of these ideas that you like. They are not mine anyhow; they are a gift from god.

Summary

Some possible names for a church as I am describing are:

1. Church of the Saviors of This World – because all of the members need to focus on saving <u>this</u> world.

2. Church of the Seekers and Finders – because we are all seekers as well as finders, all high priests as well as pa rishioners.

3. The Honeysuckle Church – because it spreads naturally and powerfully

4. The catholic Church – because it is for everyone

Chapter 40:

CONCLUSION

What I have done in this book is to say things as I see them. They provide a bedrock for my life, which is a much more powerful ground to stand on than the one I had when I was a believing Catholic. People from a strong faith background may say that I take a minimalist approach to things – we can't know about god or afterlife; we don't need him for morality, prayer, etc. In a sense I have, but it is minimal in a good sense. After you clear away all of the accretions, what is fundamental?

I hope you not only test what I say against your own experience, but that you also test whatever anybody who talks about god says against your own experience. We all do this anyhow, but a lot of people don't admit it. It is time to come out of the closet and consciously admit that we choose to judge what others have to say against our own experience. There are two things that bother me about "tradition." One is captured by a wonderful phrase that Jonathan Swift used in speaking of some writers: "because they are wondrous dark they are wondrous deep." If we can't understand something – it is "dark" – then there must be something "deep" about it. It is a "mystery" whose depth only a few privileged souls in the universe are privy to. That could be true, but it could also mean that the emperor has no clothes. It is like lawyers who are struggling to translate obtuse legal tracts into plain English. You ask, "What does this phrase, or clause or paragraph mean?" They answer, "Nobody knows!" Perhaps it pointed to a truth in antiquity, but if nobody knows, or especially if you don't know what truth it points to, then forget about it; it doesn't matter. The instinctive retort comes back, "What if there is some profound truth underneath it, that we are missing?" So what? There are profound truths everywhere. Why not seek truth in what we do know, what we do understand, rather than struggle with and agonize about what we don't understand. The universe is not limited in her vehicles for manifesting itself. Perhaps this is why my first principle (great truth/belief) is that if you can't know something, it doesn't matter.

I have two misgivings about this book. The first is that it may fall into the wrong hands – people who may be upset by it. I mean strong believers for whom their faith has provided a strong support, or who may have had a strong faith experience, which was a turning point in their lives. For example, a lot of people attribute their turning from crime, drugs or alcohol to their turning to Jesus. They may feel I am trying to destroy something precious inside of them. Of course, they are responsible for how they receive and hold everything, but they may not be at a point where they are capable of and ready to distinguish between what is essential in their experience from the wrappings through which it is experienced and expressed. Possibly it wasn't Jesus who saved them; it may be that they saved themselves, through the instrumentality of other people who had faith in them. Then again, being upset with the book may not necessarily be bad. It could be the beginning of a journey that leads one to discover more fundamental values.

The second misgiving is that I am a very rational and conceptual thinker. While editing this book I was listening to some tapes on spirituality by Ram Dass and realize that I have very little sense of some of the things he talks about. After 12 years of writing this, I had hopes that this would be a final word. I now see that it is a good beginning. My disappointment springs from my not having discovered the mysteries that the mystics, meditators, spiritualists, dreamers, metaphysicals, telepathics, saints and other seers have seemed to reach. I still find it difficult and sometimes even annoying to read their works. But I am no longer as skeptical of them as I once was. Maybe just because I don't understand something doesn't mean that there's nothing there. So, I have grown during this process!

In the past year or so in I have started participating in Holotropic workshops, and I must say that I have sometimes entered quite alternate states of consciousness. They have been profound states where I see my unity with everything in the universe. They have given me a profound compassion for all human beings. However, I am still not willing to say that I have experienced god, or the mystical. This may be what the mystics are talking about them. Maybe they are talking about the same thing that I am, but they just use different language. It also may be just the beginning of what they are talking about. In one sense everything I've written in the past 12 years is perhaps just prologue to the present, and what is best as yet to come.

However, having said all this, I am pleased with what I have produced. It has been a tremendous learning process for me. I have cleared up a lot of questions that I formerly had. I have done a wonderful purging of my entire house, and I have only essential furniture in place. It is sparse but beautiful. I feel there's nothing lacking, and I am willing to add beautifying elements to my house. I feel infinitely more on solid ground than I felt before this journey. I am so thankful for being here.

I have shared my vision of what a church based on this theology might look like. We are in charge, we are gods. If so, what's the best way to organize? If not, what's the best way to organize anyhow! When mankind firmly grasps the idea that we are sacred, that this is it and that we are in charge of this incredible playground we have been given to play on, the next stage of our flowering will occur. The times will decide whether this is an idea whose time has come or not.

Beyond Organized Religion

About Frank Sanitate Associates

Frank Sanitate is president of Frank Sanitate Associates, which he established in 1977. He and his five associates present transformational workshops for professionals. His firm has taught tens of thousands of lawyers, CPAs and other professionals over the past 25 years.

They provide a variety of workshops and resources which are listed below.

Workshops

Time Management/Time Mastery

Frank is perhaps the best known presenter of Time Management workshops for lawyers and accountants in North America. His premier workshop is:

- **Time Mastery: 60 Ways to Maximize your Productivity and Satisfaction**

Other workshops are:

Management and Human Resource Development

- The Organizational Tune-up: Communicate Better, Enjoy Work, Maximum Productivity

- The Leadership Challenge: How to Inspire, Delegate and Coach

- Management Excellence

- Don't Go To Work Unless It's Fun: How to Become Happier and More Productive

Personal Skill Development

- Shortcuts to Success: The 14 Best Tools For Personal and Professional Growth

- Triple Your Memory and Confidence, and Halve Your Stress

- Problem-Solving and Creative Thinking for the 21st Century

- Building a Successful Retirement

Communication/Conflict Resolution

- Day-to-Day Negotiation Skills: How to Produce Better Outcomes with Colleagues, Staff and Clients

- Working with Difficult People: Leading Edge Communication Skills

- Mastering the One-Minute Relationship

- Talk Your Way to the Top: Managing and Maximizing Relationships

- How to Produce Successful Outcomes in Any Conflict, Mediation or Negotiation

Effective Writing

- Effective Writing: Simplify the Process; Simplify the Product

Money Management

- Money: A Holistic Approach to Financial Independence

- What You Need to Know About Wall Street

- What You Should Know About Pension Investing (1/2 day)

- Understanding Charitable Giving

Books

This is Frank's second book. He has also published:
• *Don't Go To Work Unless It's Fun: State-of-the-Heart Time Management*

Audiotapes

The following workshops are available of audiotape.
They include 6 hours of audiotape plus a workshop manual.

• **Time Mastery: 60 Ways to Meximize Your Productivity and Satisfaction**

• **Don't Go To Work Unless It's Fun: How to Become Happier and More Productive.**

• **Effective Writing: Simplify the Process; Simplify the Product.**

Website

For more information about Frank Sanitate Associate's workshops and products, you can contact their website:

www.franksanitate.com

or contact

Frank Sanitate Associates
1135 Camino Manadero
Santa Barbara, CA 93111
(805) 967-7899